The Business
Of
Business

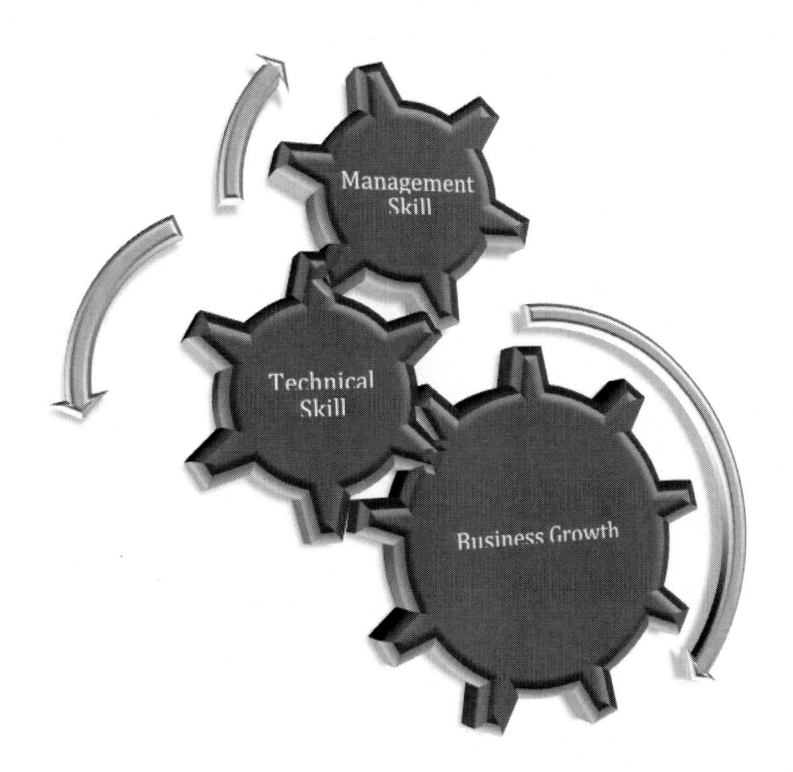

Ronald La Fournie
Calgary Alberta
www.practicalbusinesscoach.com

Copyright © 2011 by 1598290 Alberta Inc. All rights reserved. No part of this publication may be reproduced, stored in a retrieval system, or transmitted in any form or by any means without the prior written permission of the publisher, nor be otherwise circulated in any form of binding or cover other than that in which it is published and without a similar condition being imposed on the subsequent purchaser.

Published in Canada by

1598290 Alberta Inc.

Calgary, Alberta, Canada

Professional editing provided by www.Book-Editing-Services.com

www.practicalbusinesscoach.com

ISBN 978-1-257-95298-4

Do you have a business...

or a job?

```
        Plan
    ↗        ↘
Control      Organize
    ↖        ↙
      Coordinate
```

Table of Contents

Prologue 11

What People Have Said About The Practical Coach! 13

Introduction 19
    BUSINESS HEALTH CHECK UP 21

The Cause Of Most Business Problems? 27

The Solution 33
    STEP 1 – UNDERSTAND THE PROBLEM 33
    STEP 2 – WHAT DO YOU WANT TO ACCOMPLISH? 34
        Personal Direction Questionnaire 39
    STEP 3 – ARE YOU IN THE RIGHT BUSINESS? 43
        1) Do you have a profitable sale? 43
        2) Can you control your variable costs? 43
        3) Can you control your overhead costs? 43
        4) Can you sustain the sales level required? 43
    STEP 4 – LAYING OUT YOUR BUSINESS TRACK 51

Components Of A Business System 53
    1. SALES OR 'GETTING THE WORK' 54
    2. ORGANIZATION OR 'DOING THE WORK' 56
    3. FINANCIAL MANAGEMENT OR 'MEASURING THE WORK' 61
    4. MANAGEMENT OR 'CONTROLLING IT ALL' 63

What's Holding You Back? 65

Personal Action Plan 68

Management System Components 70

Understanding Financial Statements 73

The 'Dashboard' Report 93

Conclusion 95

The Manager's Tool-Box 97

Hi, I'm Ron La Fournie, and I developed my unique approach to business through a lifetime of learning and coaching, beginning with a degree in economics from the University of Lethbridge in Lethbridge Alberta, Canada. I also taught the university karate club as a black belt instructor (course I was a little younger then).

I learned my practical business approach during 40 years of experience in which I:

- ☑ operated my own small business (trucking)

- ☑ worked as a general manager for a large international retail business ($5,000,000 in annual revenue with 43 employees)

- ☑ worked with the Federal Business Development Bank in Lethbridge, Calgary and Edmonton as a commercial loans officer and also played a major role in developing their seminar training program. I also organized the annual 'Small Business Week Trade show' in Calgary for several years

- ☑ as a member of the Calgary Chamber of Commerce I chaired the 'Education Committee' for two years and organized numerous workshops and seminars

- ☑ was the president of 'The Independent Business Institute' in Calgary and authored a management training program titled 'Practical Management Skills' that was co-sponsored with 'Price-Waterhouse' and 'Mount Royal College' and marketed to the business public

- ☑ spent 13 years as a senior project manager for a large international U. S. based consulting firm specializing in business turn-a-rounds with clients all over North America

- ☑ spent a year as the general manager of a Calgary manufacturing company during which my task was to build a solid management team and establish international distributors in the Middle East, Egypt, Russia, and Colombia

- ☑ I am now semi retired, which just means I work a bit less, and play a lot more

Prologue

Several years ago I was watching a football game when a commercial aired that really made me sit up and watch. It opened with a boy of about six or seven years riding on a school bus and drawing on his Etch-A-Sketch. He was drawing a dinosaur and all I could see at first was an outline. As the school bus passed stop after stop, I saw the drawing take shape and become very detailed. By the time he reached his stop he had the most incredibly detailed drawing of a dinosaur and I was amazed that a boy of his age could do such a work of art.

He then stands and moves toward the exit when he suddenly stumbles and shakes up his Etch-A-Sketch. He looks at his drawing with an absolute expression of horror as he realizes his Etch-A-Sketch is now blank.... his drawing, and all his work, is gone!

What made me sit up and take notice was the realization that many of my clients, and other business owners and managers operate their business in the same way as this little boy managed his art work...'all the critical information is maintained in a manner that can be easily lost'.

In short, they keep it in their heads, and every once in while *something* happens to cause a 'stumble' or a 'bump', and *something* is lost or forgotten. This *something* that is lost or forgotten or that falls through the cracks...**always costs money**.

It might be an appointment that is forgotten, a phone call you were supposed to return, a germ of a sales idea, or something with an employee. Many individuals have told me they often lay awake at night running through a mental list of things they must do tomorrow, or the next day.

It doesn't matter how bright or how smart you are...nobody can remember everything. And just trying can lead to a very stressful situation.

I started to call this approach 'Etch-A-Sketch Management'. And every time I mention the story to a client, they immediately know what I am getting at and can identify with the boy's horror at the loss of all the work. They keep everything about their business in their heads or on dozens of post-it notes and are constantly forgetting and losing them, or are constantly afraid they'll forget something.

Does that ring a bell?

What People Have Said About The Practical Coach!

> "Ron has led a number of consulting engagements at my company each with the goal of making us more efficient and profitable. His vast experience and knowledge working with all kinds of businesses allow him to quickly find the constraints within a company and come up with creative problem solving ways to move business forward more efficiently and profitably. I would highly recommend Ron to anyone looking to improve his/her business."
>
> Patrick Finn
> President, Patrick A. Finn Ltd. (New Home Construction, Chicago Illinois)

Reprinted from http://www.linkedin.com

> I had the pleasure of working with Ron at various client companies. Ron is an effective communicator and analyst. He has the unique ability to see through all the chaos and get to the heart of the issues facing an ailing company. Ron's ability to provide coaching and guidance to me as I tackled on site issues was always invaluable to me. The bottom line is that Ron is not only able to provide answers, but is able to implement change to save companies on the brink. I would recommend Ron to any potential client and would work with Ron any chance I got."
>
> Jed Black
>
> Business Manager/Controller at 'The Who We Are Counts Institute LLC.' Kingsport Tennessee.

Reprinted from http://www.linkedin.com

WORLD OIL TOOLS INC.

March 21, 2011

RE: Reference Letter for Ronald LaFournie

To Whom it may concern:

I had the pleasure of working with Ron LaFournie at World Oil Tools for the period March 2010 to March 2011.

During this period, Mr. LaFournie was the General Manager of World Oil Tools, and I was part of the senior management team that reported directly to him.

I enjoyed working with Ron, and found Ron to be an outstanding manager. He is very adept at driving change within an organization, and was able to create a vision that helped to motivate individuals, and drive the organization forward. I personally believe that one of Ron's greatest strengths is that fact that he does not micromanage any of his direct reports. He is an excellent listener; he listens carefully to his staff, takes their suggestions, discusses the issues and concerns, and then allows them to proceed on their task with his full support. He essentially allows his employees to do the jobs they were hired to do

From an interpersonal perspective, I found Ron to be very ethical, intelligent, and in addition, he had a great sense of humor.

Please feel free to contact me with any questions you may have, or if further information is required, as I would strongly recommend Ron to any organization.

I can be reached at (403) 870-4149, or (403) 257-1132.

Sincerely,

Foster Wright, MBA
Chief Financial Officer
World Oil Tools Inc.

Bay 6, 3504 – 72 Avenue S.E. Calgary, Alberta, Canada T2C 1J9
Telephone: (403) 720-5155 Fax: (403) 720-5156
Web page: www.worldoiltools.com

Ever-Clear Property Services Inc.
#111, 519-34th Avenue S.E.
Calgary, Alberta
T2G 1V1
Ph: 259-2468 / Fax: 243-0267

June 16, 2011

Mr. Ron La Fournie

The Business Coach, Ron, has taken me from the dark ages and shown me that anything's possible. Besides being very personable and knowledgeable, Ron has taught me the skills I needed to bring my employees and my business to the next level. We're still in the planning stages but WOW!!, I am excited for what the future holds.

Thanks Ron,

Bill Allen

President
Everclear Property Services Inc.
billallen@everclearinc.ca

Bob Wallace Excavating Ltd.
Box 201, DeWinton, Alberta T0L-0X0
Phone 403-804-8000 • 403 257-7679
Email - bobwallaceexcavating@xplornet.ca
www.bobwallaceexcavating.ca

June 22, 2011

Testimonial:

My husband and I hired Ron as a Business Coach to determine if we were a viable business and if we could make a profit and not just break-even every month.

After four months of working with Ron, we know we are a viable business and we can make a good profit and not just break-even. Ron was able to determine our deficiencies from the start. Ron helped us understand our Profit and Loss statements so we know how much overhead and margin we need to charge for each job.

Ron has provided us many tools and skills, too many too mention, one in particular is a template to quote properly for each job, which is truly amazing, as well as a Cash Flow sheet specific to our company that I now work with on a regular basis, which allows me to see all transactions of cash in and out on monthly basis.

In closing, I cannot say enough about how Ron got us on track. Ron is a very good teacher and talked to us in layman's terms to understand what we needed to know to operate a good business.

I can now see the potential with our company and I am very excited where we will go in the future. We look forward to further coaching with you in the Future.

Thanks Ron, have a great summer!

Laurie and Bob Wallace

Introduction

This book has been written for people who run their own business that have not had formal business education or been trained as managers. It will help them learn the basics in order to survive and even grow a little more successful.

If you are one of these individuals you may feel:

- that your business is out of control,
- that you really do not know how to manage,
- that it's not what you thought it would be,
- that some of your employees make more money than you,
- that your family life is suffering,
- that there is a lot of stress,
- the stress is causing other health problems,
- that you're a failure,
- that it's just not fun anymore,
- that you want some help…but just don't know where to turn,
- that you're doing ok, but want a second opinion or just want to make sure you aren't missing something.

If any of these things apply then this is for you!

The 'Business of Business' is simple, it's about making money. It's about knowing what to measure and how to interpret the measurements.

I suggest you complete the Business Health Check-Up following in order to set a benchmark or starting point. It will indicate management areas where your knowledge is lacking and help you determine your priorities.

Business Health Check Up

This questionnaire consists of 63 questions and should not take more than 20 minutes of your time. Once completed you can score yourself and your business and read the appropriate section of the Health Report. This will be your evaluation of your business. But do be honest with yourself as the purpose of the questionnaire is to become aware of areas where you can improve your management skills.

General			
Do you feel in control of your business?	Yes ☐	No ☐	Don't Know ☐
Do you have enough free time for your family?	Yes ☐	No ☐	Don't Know ☐
Are you making enough money?	Yes ☐	No ☐	Don't Know ☐
Do you have a written business plan?	Yes ☐	No ☐	Don't Know ☐
Are you a good manager?	Yes ☐	No ☐	Don't Know ☐
Do you know what your strengths are?	Yes ☐	No ☐	Don't Know ☐
Do you know what your weaknesses are?	Yes ☐	No ☐	Don't Know ☐
Do you work too much?	Yes ☐	No ☐	Don't Know ☐
Are you still having fun running your business?	Yes ☐	No ☐	Don't Know ☐
Is the stress level getting too high?	Yes ☐	No ☐	Don't Know ☐
Sales and Marketing			
Do you have enough sales?	Yes ☐	No ☐	Don't Know ☐
Are your prices competitive?	Yes ☐	No ☐	Don't Know ☐
Is your pricing based on your cost structure?	Yes ☐	No ☐	Don't Know ☐
Do you have specific target markets?	Yes ☐	No ☐	Don't Know ☐
Have you identified customer benefits?	Yes ☐	No ☐	Don't Know ☐
Do you know how customers perceive your company?	Yes ☐	No ☐	Don't Know ☐
Do you know your competition?	Yes ☐	No ☐	Don't Know ☐
Do you have a sales strategy?	Yes ☐	No ☐	Don't Know ☐
Do you have a sales action plan?	Yes ☐	No ☐	Don't Know ☐
Do you have a sales activity tracking system?	Yes ☐	No ☐	Don't Know ☐
Do you have a sales incentive plan?	Yes ☐	No ☐	Don't Know ☐
Do you have an advertising budget?	Yes ☐	No ☐	Don't Know ☐
Does your advertising work?	Yes ☐	No ☐	Don't Know ☐
Do your sales people maximize your revenue?	Yes ☐	No ☐	Don't Know ☐
Are they constantly being trained to improve?	Yes ☐	No ☐	Don't Know ☐

Organization			
Is your workflow efficient?	Yes ☐	No ☐	Don't Know ☐
Do you know how productive your employees are?	Yes ☐	No ☐	Don't Know ☐
Do they do their jobs the way you want them to?	Yes ☐	No ☐	Don't Know ☐
Are your people accountable for what they do?	Yes ☐	No ☐	Don't Know ☐
Do you have job descriptions for each position?	Yes ☐	No ☐	Don't Know ☐
Do you have good communication in your business?	Yes ☐	No ☐	Don't Know ☐
Do you have difficulty hiring the right people?	Yes ☐	No ☐	Don't Know ☐
Do you have an employee evaluation system?	Yes ☐	No ☐	Don't Know ☐
Do employees clearly understand your expectations?	Yes ☐	No ☐	Don't Know ☐
Do you compare actual results with set standards?	Yes ☐	No ☐	Don't Know ☐
Operations			
Do you have a purchasing program?	Yes ☐	No ☐	Don't Know ☐
Do you know what a purchasing program is?	Yes ☐	No ☐	Don't Know ☐
Do you know what your inventory turnover rate is?	Yes ☐	No ☐	Don't Know ☐
Do jobs move through without snags and problems?	Yes ☐	No ☐	Don't Know ☐
Do you have re-work?	Yes ☐	No ☐	Don't Know ☐
Do employees ever waste time?	Yes ☐	No ☐	Don't Know ☐
Are you getting a good return on labor investment?	Yes ☐	No ☐	Don't Know ☐
Do you have a quality control program?	Yes ☐	No ☐	Don't Know ☐
Do you know how to motivate your staff?	Yes ☐	No ☐	Don't Know ☐

Financial			
Do you always have enough cash in the bank?	Yes☐	No☐	Don't Know☐
Are accounts receivable where they should be?	Yes☐	No☐	Don't Know☐
Do you ever forget to send out an invoice?	Yes☐	No☐	Don't Know☐
Do you pay your bills too fast?	Yes☐	No☐	Don't Know☐
Do you ever pay an invoice twice?	Yes☐	No☐	Don't Know☐
Do you have a cash management system?	Yes☐	No☐	Don't Know☐
Do you know how you're doing at any given point?	Yes☐	No☐	Don't Know☐
Do you get financial reports?	Yes☐	No☐	Don't Know☐
Do you understand them?	Yes☐	No☐	Don't Know☐
Do they give you the information you want?	Yes☐	No☐	Don't Know☐
Are there other things you would like to track?	Yes☐	No☐	Don't Know☐
Are you happy with your gross profit?	Yes☐	No☐	Don't Know☐
Are you controlling your overhead ratio?	Yes☐	No☐	Don't Know☐
Do you know how to calculate it?	Yes☐	No☐	Don't Know☐
Do you know how much profit you need?	Yes☐	No☐	Don't Know☐
Do you have a budget?	Yes☐	No☐	Don't Know☐
Do you have an accurate bidding/estimating system?	Yes☐	No☐	Don't Know☐
Do you know your break-even point?	Yes☐	No☐	Don't Know☐
Can you use it as a decision making tool?	Yes☐	No☐	Don't Know☐

Now ask yourself…Do I really know the answers?…or am I just guessing? Are my answers honest?…**or just what I would like them to be?**

Scoring-count answers as indicated below!

# of Yes Answers   _____
# of No Answers   _____
# of Don't Know Answers   _____
        Total   63

# of No & Don't Knows_____/63 = _____%

Total # of questions (63). Now divide the total of No and Don't Know answers by 63 to obtain a percentage rating. For example 25 No's + 22 Don't Knows = 47
      47 divided by 63 = 74.6%

Health Report

No & Don't Know % Rate	Explanation	Solution
20% or Less	You are fairly healthy, but could lose a few pounds and should exercise more while watching your diet. There are some minor infections that can be treated with specific drugs. No life threatening conditions exist.	Take An Aspirin
20 % to 30%	You have the early warning signs of high blood pressure, increased cholesterol levels, and are susceptible to chronic colds and flu symptoms. Cosmetic surgery is not an option here, rather a strict regimen of therapy is recommended, and a second opinion might be very prudent (consultants might be very effective at this stage).	Get A Prescription
30% to 40%	You are in eminent danger of a heart attack and need to schedule bypass surgery sometime in the next few months.	Schedule Surgery
40% to 75%	You are hemorrhaging and better call the ambulance to get you into the emergency room for immediate surgery. No time for second opinions.	Head to the emergency room right now!
75% and up	Call your lawyer to update your will and make sure the insurance premiums are paid! CPR is needed NOW! Get A Job!	You're heading for the morgue!

The above represents only a cursory self-examination resulting from a very preliminary review, but I hope you get the point. If you are in excess of 30% of No and Don't Know answers you're heading for trouble.

Do something before it's too late.

Now What?

Health Report Solutions	Real World Meaning
Take an aspirin	Look closely at all your costs and determine where you can cut or trim needless expenses. Plug the leaks before looking for more sales.
Get a prescription	Update or complete a business plan. Then follow it!
Schedule surgery	Have an independent expert analyze your operations and suggest improvements.
Head to the emergency room right now!	You need to get into survival mode and only a turn around specialist can help you.
You're heading for the morgue!	Not everyone is suited to running a business. You will make more per hour and have less stress working for someone else.

The Cause Of Most Business Problems?

Most serious problems in business, and most business failures occur because people make a fatal assumption …

They assume:

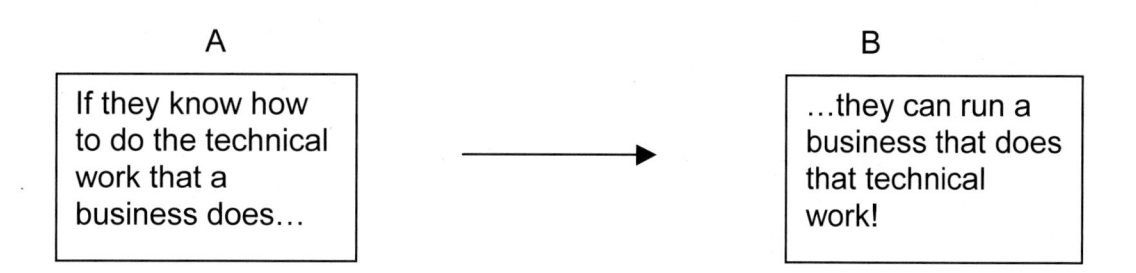

A
| If they know how to do the technical work that a business does… |

⟶

B
| …they can run a business that does that technical work! |

Let me give you an example.

You have good skills at a trade such as plumbing, carpentry, electrical, photography, HVAC, engineering, architecture, floral arrangements and so on. You are tired of working for someone else and likely have dreamt of owning your own business for years. Because you are very good at doing the work (Box A) you assume that you can run a business that does that work (Box B).

It's exciting. You talk it over with your spouse and friends who encourage you. So, off you go to the bank to borrow money to buy the necessary equipment and vehicles to get started. The bank wants a business plan. HUH, what's a business plan? No big problem really: the bank gives you an outline to follow and you complete it to their satisfaction…I mean, you want the loan, right? And of course the bank needs to take a second mortgage on your home, or asks for someone to co-sign the loan. This is your dream, so you go ahead…. The bank approves your loan and…

Voila you're a businessperson, right?

WRONG!!!

After a short time you find yourself worrying about:

> - hiring people to do what you used to do,
> - trying to get them to do it the way you used to do it,
> - dealing with their constant problems of getting the work done on time, (ever feel like you're running an adult day care center?)
> - having money for payroll, and why are you last to get paid?
> - having enough money to buy more inventory,
> - being pressured by the people to whom you owe money, for inventory you bought previously,
> - trying to figure out how to get more sales,
> - finding time to spend getting more sales,
> - trying to collect the money owed to you from previous sales,
> - having money to pay all the bills on time,
> - having to send the government the money you withheld on payroll,
> - trying to figure out where all the money goes,
> - where is all the money my Profit & Loss statement says I am making?
> - if I'm so busy, why don't I have any money?

One day you realize you have started to work longer and longer hours, the stress is building, you can't sleep at nights, and your family life is starting to suffer.

This is not why you wanted your own business. You continue to do more and more of what you are good at--<u>the technical work</u>—and you work harder and harder just to stay in the same place, but still don't seem to be getting anywhere.

What happened to the fun of the early days?

<u>You sometimes think you can probably go back to work for someone else and make more money!</u>

Well, if you notice there is **gap** between Box A and Box B.

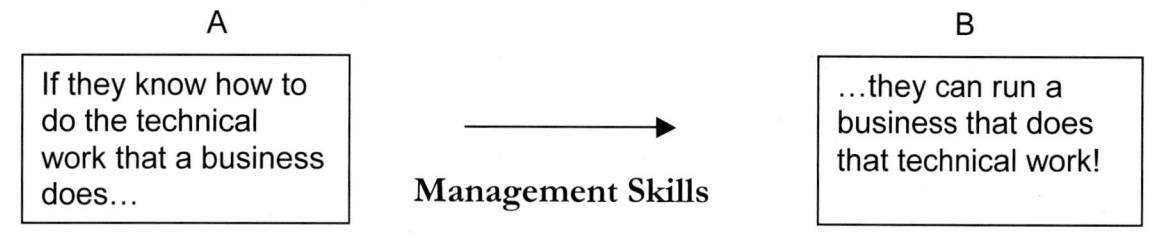

A		B
If they know how to do the technical work that a business does…	⎯⎯⎯⎯➤ **Management Skills**	…they can run a business that does that technical work!

That **gap** is where management skills fit. This is simply knowing how to plan and control your business in order to deal with the things you didn't know how to deal with when you started.

Remember the earlier list of issues:

- hiring people to do what you used to do,
- trying to get them to do it the way you used to do it,
- dealing with their constant problems of getting the work done on time, (ever feel like you're running an adult day care center?)
- having money for payroll, and why are you last to get paid?
- having enough money to buy more inventory,
- being pressured by the people to whom you owe money, for inventory you bought previously,
- trying to figure out how to get more sales,
- finding time to spend getting more sales,
- trying to collect the money owed to you from previous sales,
- having money to pay all the bills on time,
- having to send the government the money you withheld on payroll,
- trying to figure out where all the money goes,

> where is all the money my Profit & Loss statement says I am making?

if I'm so busy, why don't I have any money?

Fortunately management is a skill and because it is a skill it is learnable and transferable from one person to another. <u>If you can think systematically, you can learn the basics well enough to continue to operate or even to save your business.</u>

I have found that most of the people that run a business because they are good at the technical side are also good systematic thinkers.

Engineers often have difficulties trying to be perfect, and then can't figure out why they can't make money! Quality control does not mean being perfect, it just means adherence to a set of standards. Plumbers have to follow a logical process, contractors have to build in a logical order. For instance you can't drywall before the electrician is finished, and you can't paint before the drywall, taping and sanding is finished. Seems like common sense right? Well, running a business is 'kinda' like that too.

<u>You need to look at it as a system, then identify the tools you need and learn how to use them.</u>

The bank's business plan would have included very little of this information about how you should actually run your business on a day-to-day basis, it would have included things they needed to know in order to decide if they should lend you money, and how to protect themselves if you failed. Business gurus sell you all kind of materials (books, tapes & videos) that tell you what to do…but not how to do it!

'The Business of Business' is about helping you learn those management skills and day-to-day activities to fill the gap between Box A and Box B.

Do you have a business…..or just a job?

Company staff should spend their working time as broken out below. An owner should spend most of the time doing the strategic work, planning how and where to improve sales, how to improve the way in which the actual work is done in order to increase efficiencies, how to price in order to improve margins and profit. An owner should only spend a small amount of time actually doing the work of the business.

Strategic is the planning part, 'Tactical' is the actual doing of the work.

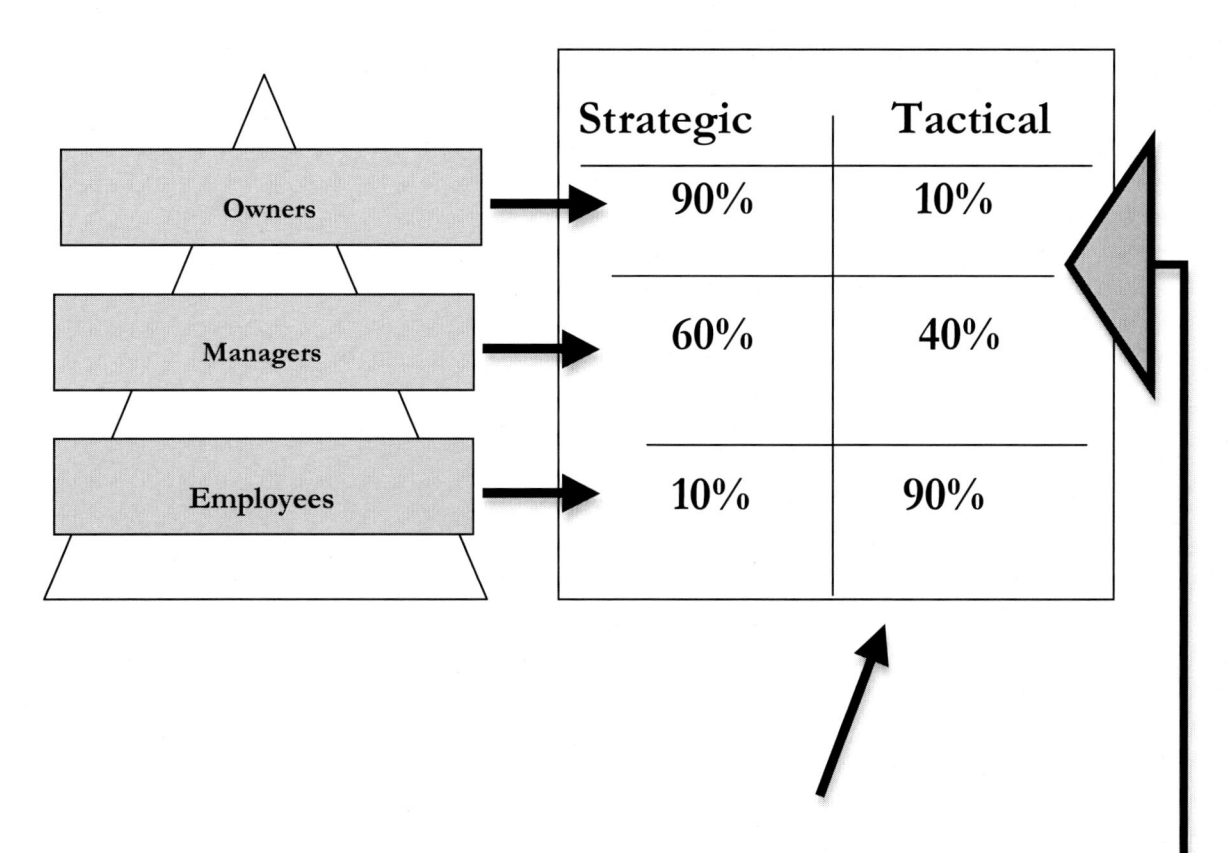

	Strategic	Tactical
Owners	90%	10%
Managers	60%	40%
Employees	10%	90%

If you did not do well in the 'Business Health Check-Up' you likely spend most of your time in the lowest box in the tactical column above.

You're working hard at what you are good at doing, and that's 'Working In The Business'. That is doing the work of your business. And as a result of this no one is 'Working On The Business' in the top level of the Strategic column above.

The Solution

Step 1 – Understand The Problem

My purpose in this book is to show some of the things you need to learn, and then coach you through doing it while you're running your business.

To begin, you first must recognize that:

> **Problems cannot be solved at the same level of awareness that created them.**

In other words, **you** need to learn some new skills. If **you** decide not to change, then **you** will not change the fatal assumption mentioned earlier and **you** will continue with the same problems. This is doing nothing. Think about the cost of doing nothing. Things just continue as they are!

Is that acceptable?

If so, stop reading, put this book down, and go back to the way you have been doing things!

If you decide you want to change and fix the problems with your business you must first:

1. Ensure you are at least operating in a survival mode
2. Learn to understand 'The Business of Business'
3. Build a business structure
4. Learn to understand and implement fundamental controls

In this way **you** will no longer be assuming **you** understand how to run your business...**you** will actually learn to understand how to run your business, and **you** will no longer be a victim of the fatal assumption.

Step 2 – What Do You Want To Accomplish?

We have all seen movies where an athlete pictures in his or her mind the result they would like to achieve. A golfer pictures his swing and the flight of the ball. A high jumper pictures his or her approach and jump. A gymnast pictures her run-up and world class jump or vault. They do this over and over again prior to competition…and it helps to improve their performance.

They are people, just like you and I. Some of us do the same thing when we are playing golf or baseball. And if we do it consistently, it does help.

Many years ago when I was an employee and just starting to work as a business consultant, I was continually talking about what it would be like to drive a Corvette. It was a dream and I never thought I would actually have one of my very own.

One day my wife came home with a brochure she had picked up at a dealership. I wanted a red one so she had cut out a large glossy picture of a red Corvette and made me put it in the front of my day-timer. This made me look at it every day, and after a few weeks of seeing this and my wife asking me each day what I had done that day to move closer to buying it, a funny thing happened…I found myself planning the little steps to move in that direction.

Not too many months later I took possession of my very own little red Corvette - it was a dream come true! Only then did I start to appreciate the effectiveness of picturing goals.

I now know that…

> # We move toward and become like that 'which we think about'.

This is true whether we think about positive or negative things.

But when we start our own business we forget about the mental images of doing something well, we forget about the big picture. We think that picturing our goals is for athletes…and that it has nothing to do with running a business anyway.

Most businesses struggle just to make a living…never mind making any serious money. And they struggle because they continue to believe in the 'fatal assumption'.

You must clearly know what you want.

> Do you want to make a specific amount of money?
> Do you want to be able to retire at a certain time?
> Do you want to work at something with your family?
> Do you want something to leave your family?
> Do you want to buy your son or daughter their first car?
> Do you want to go on a vacation?
> Do you want to own property?
> Do you want to buy a Corvette?

Write what you want in the box below.

Only you can answer these questions, and there is no right or wrong answer. Your goals are your own. But they must be realistic and consider the business you are in. And they must be measurable by some type of yardstick: dollars, time, months, years, etc.

If you cannot measure it, you cannot manage it!

Now, sit back and close your eyes.

Picture what your life will be like when you accomplish your goal. Describe it in the box below.

| |
| |

Looks pretty good doesn't it?

Now decide how bad you really want it. How committed are you to getting there?

On a scale of 1-10, with 10 being the highest, circle your commitment level:

| 1 | 2 | 3 | 4 | 5 | 6 | 7 | 8 | 9 | 10 |

Personal Direction Questionnaire

The purpose of this "Personal Direction" Questionnaire is to help you determine where your personal/family status, goals and objectives mesh with your role as part of a closely held company and an active employee.

The direction you desire to pursue personally has an influence on the direction of the organization and your role in it. While we do not want to allow the business to run your life, as an employee your personal goals must be compatible with the company's. This information also should be part of the basis for the Long Term Goals for both yourself and your organization.

1. What are the major contributions you personally make to the company?

A)

B)

C)

D)

2. What do you, or would you, like to do with your personal time; outside the organization? (Specifically, what hobbies do you, or would you, care to pursue, other business ventures, travel, etc?)

A)

B)

C)

3. How would you like to see your time allocation changing over the next two to three years as a percent of your total available time. Place the percent of your waking hours spent on each area indicated, with each column being equal to 100% of your available time.

% of Time Spent by Endeavor in:

Time Spent	now	In 1 yr	In 2 yrs	In 3 yrs
At work				
Work outside of office				
Other business				
Personal with family				
Personal Private				
Total	100%	100%	100%	100%

4. How would you rate your own skills as a businessperson in this environment? Indicate your choice with a number in the appropriate box to show what you think:

   1   You are at this level and Improving.
   2   You are at this level and Getting Worse.
   3   You are at this level and Remaining The Same.

General Proficiency	Industry Knowledge	Customer Relations	Technical Ability	Administrative Management
Excellent				
Very good				
Good				
Poor				
None				

5. What do you feel your current capacity could translate to, in terms of sales and/or production per year? Current capacity means with existing people and the existing plant and equipment.

   $

6. What are your own goals for personal net worth in two (2) years and in three (3) years?

   2 Years $ 3 Years $

7. What do you realistically think your goal for total personal compensation as a per cent of sales should be over the next three (3) years as compared to the total amount of net company profitability?

	Personal	Corporate
1st Year		
2nd Year		
3rd Year		

8. Describe your personal financial needs, in dollars, over the next three years. Only include YOUR contribution to each, not spouses, if any.

	House	Entertainment & Travel	Food	Investment	Education & Training	Medical & Health	Total
20							
20							
20							

9. When do you plan to, or would you like to retire, seek greater career or personal opportunities, leave the area for a better quality of life? If applicable, when and how do you plan to transfer any portion, or all, of the stock/shares in the business?

10. How do you define your relationship and role within the company?

11. How would you define your relationship with the other family members? Do you respect and admire them and the contribution they make to the company's overall success as well as your own?

12. Do you anticipate a change in these relationships over time? To what extent and to what result?

13. Any other comments on your personal or organizational goal(s) that you feel will help?

Step 3 – Are You In The Right Business?

Once you have your goals clear in your mind, and written down, you must determine whether or not your business can provide the means to achieve those goals. Are the goals realistic, or is it just a pipedream?

This question gives rise to four others.

1) Do you have a profitable sale?

> Most people do not know the true cost of buying or producing the product or service they sell! This is because they do not understand the scorekeeping system of business (bookkeeping) from a management perspective. They may know some part of the cost, and then they increase that by some factor. Some people double it, triple, or use some other factor. I have seen many, many different approaches. But they are all just a guess.
>
> Sometimes it works and they make money for a short time. But remember, they do not know or understand their true costs. I have witnessed this approach in all kinds of companies from small construction firms to architectural companies.

2) Can you control your variable costs?

> If you do not know what your real costs are, how can you control them? This area measures how well you do in the buying and selling of your products or services.

3) Can you control your overhead costs?

> This is almost always the area most neglected in small and medium sized businesses. This measures how well you do at running your business.

4) Can you sustain the sales level required?

> Once you know what the above cost levels are, you must determine whether or not you can achieve the needed sales level to meet these costs and to provide the required profit level. How much profit is required? Again, most business owners cannot answer this question because they do not know what profit has to pay for.

Do you know what your profit has to pay for?

The Business Of Business

I used to be amazed at the number of individuals running businesses that could not answer these questions. Now I know it's more common than not.

Let's start with the concept of Break-Even. Most of you have heard the term, and some may have used it. But do you really understand it? If you do, can you describe it, and what you might use it for? Try before you continue.

Understanding Break-Even

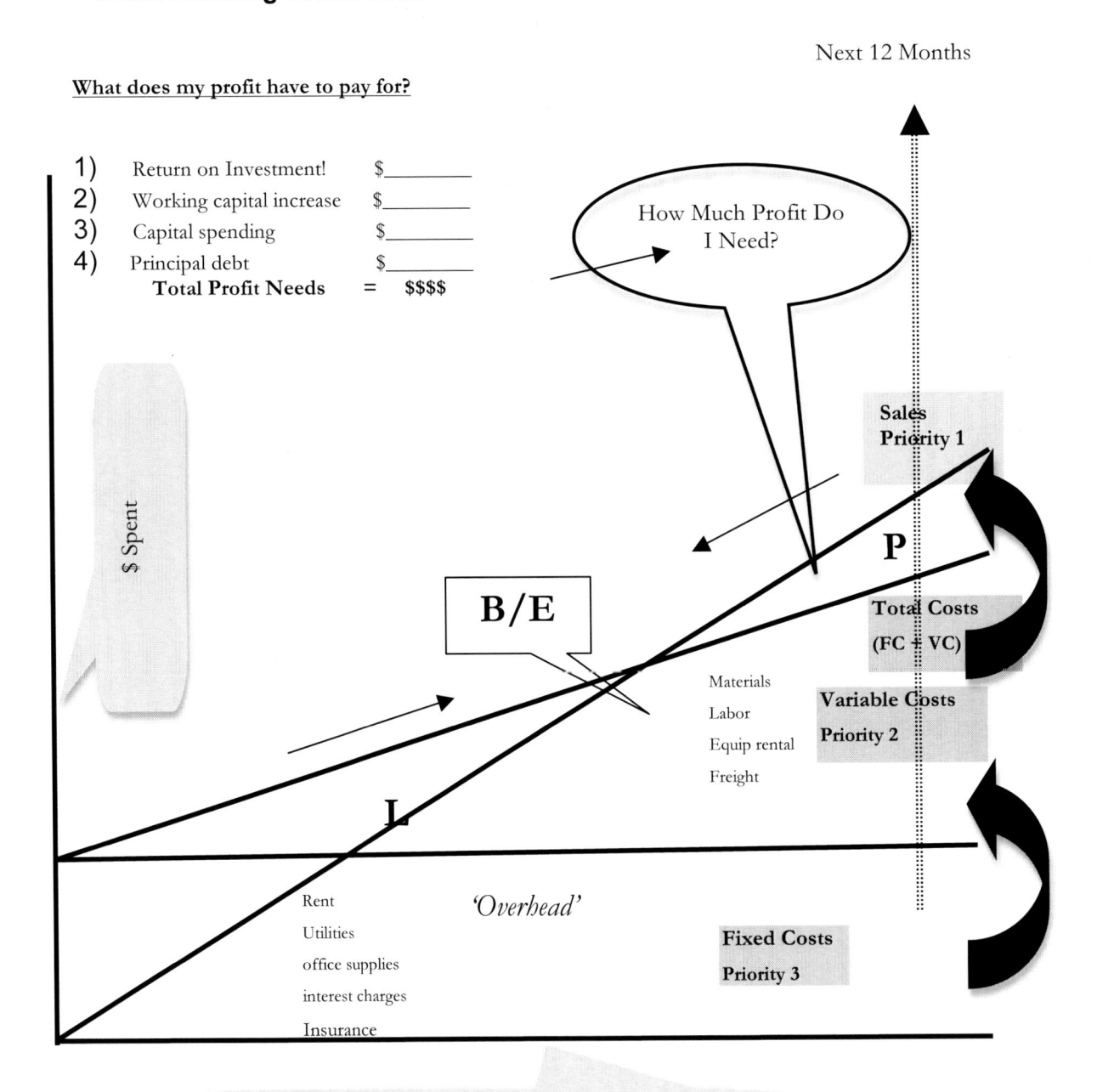

Next 12 Months

<u>What does my profit have to pay for?</u>

1) Return on Investment! $_____
2) Working capital increase $_____
3) Capital spending $_____
4) Principal debt $_____
   Total Profit Needs   = $$$$

How Much Profit Do I Need?

$ Spent

B/E

Materials
Labor
Equip rental
Freight

Rent
Utilities
office supplies
interest charges
Insurance

'Overhead'

Sales
Priority 1

P

Total Costs
(FC + VC)

Variable Costs
Priority 2

Fixed Costs
Priority 3

Time Spent

Practical Tools For Practical People

At first glance the diagram on the opposite page looks pretty complicated, but it's not really.

We are measuring Dollars ($) Spent on the vertical axis and Time Spent on the horizontal axis. In other words you spend increasing amounts of money as you go through the year. I think you will agree that you should know what you spend it on!

Start at the bottom with the Fixed Costs (F/C) or overhead. These are all the costs you have to pay whether you sell anything or not. They are indirect or not tied to any specific sale. I am sure you can relate to the examples listed.

Moving up, the variable costs (VC) are those you incur when you sell a product or a service and are those things you provide for a specific client or customer. These increase with volume; the higher your sales go, the higher the variable costs go. So, on the diagram the variable cost line slopes upward to the right.

Adding the fixed costs and the variable costs gives you the total costs. Sales starts at 0 and increases. If you follow the sales line from the bottom left corner up to the right where it meets the total cost line, you will note that intersection point is the break-even point. No profit and no loss. Below that point you are losing money, beyond it you are making profit. We can calculate this point for each day, each week, each month or per square footage of display space in a retail situation.

How much profit do you need?

As stated earlier, I have never had anyone give me the full answer to that question because they haven't realized what profit needs to cover. Those four things are listed on the diagram and are the result of having specific measureable goals and then doing the math.

If you build a product or provide a service, you have a pretty solid picture in your mind of what it will look like when you're finished. You can do the same with your business.

Looking ahead 12 months we can complete a 'financial operating plan' or a budget. If we are realistic and actually achieve the sales goal (#1 on the chart), while maintaining the relationships with the variable costs (#2 on the chart), and the fixed costs (#3 on the chart), the projected profit must be there. It's a mathematical certainty.

Since most bookkeepers don't understand Break-Even from the management perspective, they don't provide management with the right tools. Most Profit and Loss (P & L) Statements are presented without separating the fixed costs from the variable costs.

The Break-Even point is one of the best decision making tools in the management toolbox. An understanding of Break-Even will help improve your abilities tremendously. There will be no more guessing about costs and what your selling price should be…and then hoping things will work out.

Here's an example of how businesses all over North America price their products and services.

They start with what they know; the cost of labor and the cost of materials or services.

Labor	$200.00
+ Materials	$250.00
Sub-Total	450.00

Then they add a 'factor' for profit and overhead, and that's how they arrive at their selling price. The 'Factor' is sometimes 10%, 25%, 50%, 100%, 200% or more. I have seen everything you can imagine.

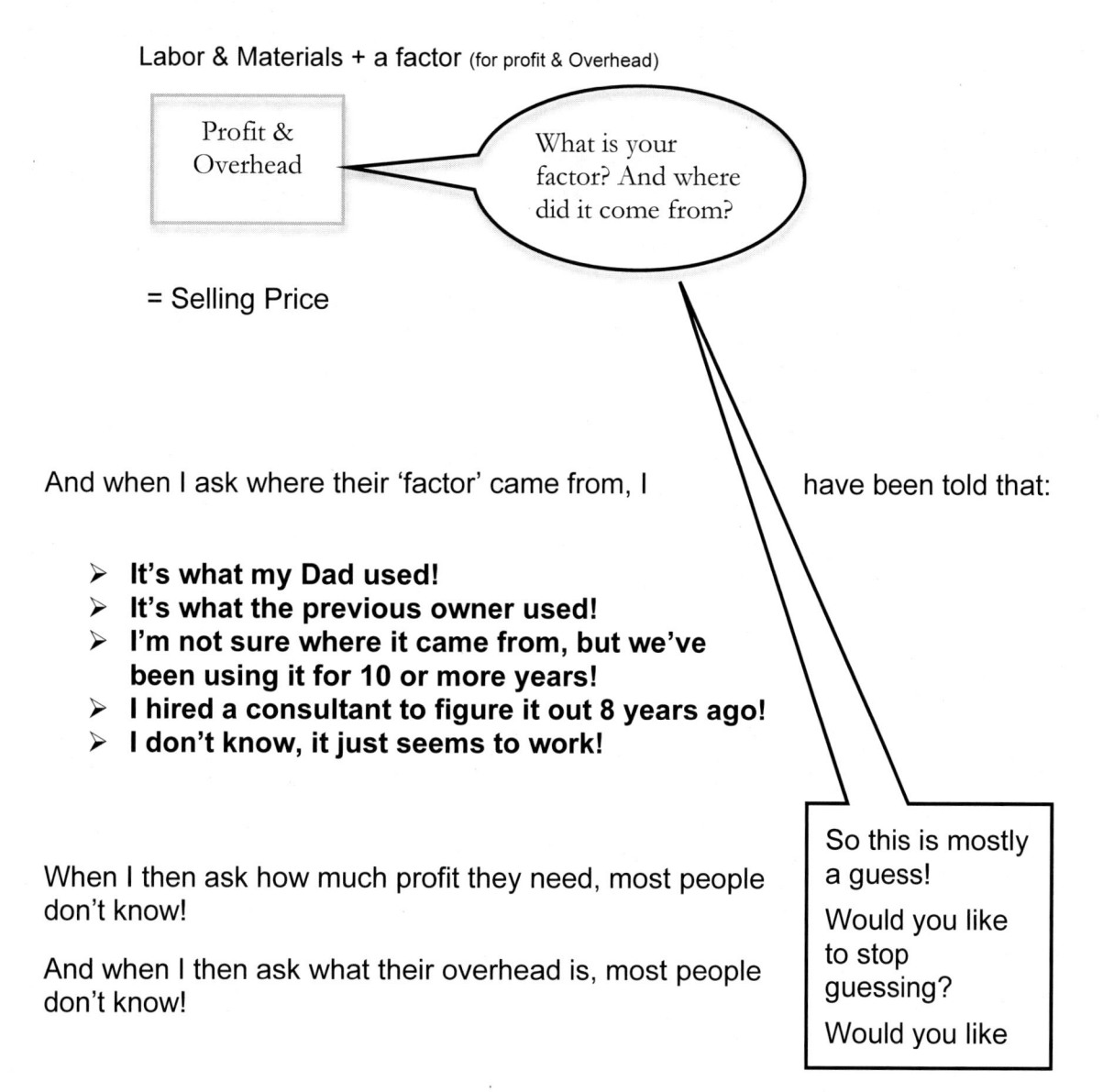

Labor & Materials + a factor (for profit & Overhead)

| Profit & Overhead | What is your factor? And where did it come from? |

= Selling Price

And when I ask where their 'factor' came from, I have been told that:

- It's what my Dad used!
- It's what the previous owner used!
- I'm not sure where it came from, but we've been using it for 10 or more years!
- I hired a consultant to figure it out 8 years ago!
- I don't know, it just seems to work!

So this is mostly a guess!

Would you like to stop guessing?

Would you like

When I then ask how much profit they need, most people don't know!

And when I then ask what their overhead is, most people don't know!

So the factor is most often a guess. They have to guess because they are not getting the right information from their people or their system and they (you) don't know what to ask for!

Understand it first, then plan it and then do it!

The Business Of Business

Example....

    I sell pens that cost me $.50 each for $1.
    I rent a booth in a mall that costs me $10.00 per week.
    There are no other costs.

How many pens do I have to sell to cover my costs? _____
That's my break-even point.

Each pen contributes $.50 towards profit, but I don't have any profit until I cover the booth rental cost for the week. That is called profit contribution, or contribution margin.

Item	Quantity	Total Sales
Pens	20	$20.00
Cost of pens	20	-$10.00
Cost of Booth	1	-$10.00
Result	Break Even	$0.00

If I want a $10.00 profit in the same week, how many pens do I have to sell? The cost of the booth is $10.00 and each pen sold contributes $.50 toward the target.

So, lets divide the target ($10.00 for the booth and $10.00 for profit =$20.00) by $.50 and we arrive at 40 pens.

Item	Quantity		Total Sales
Pens	40		$40.00
Cost of pens	40		-$20.00
Cost of Booth	1		-$10.00
Result		Profit	$10.00

Practical Tools For Practical People

Now I hire some help and I pay 20% sales commission, my costs are:

Fixed costs are still $10.00 for the booth

Variable costs are:

    $.50 for each pen

    $.20 sales commission for each pen

    So each pen sold now has a contribution margin of $.30

How many pens do I need to sell to reach Break-Even? We need to divide the fixed costs by the contribution margin.

$10.00 divided by $.30 = 33.33 pens. Now I realize you can't sell 1/3 of a pen, but follow along for the illustration of the principle.

Item	Quantity	Total Sales
Pens	33.33	$33.33
Cost of pens	33.33	-$16.67
Cost of Booth	1	-$10.00
Sales Commission	33.33	-$6.67
Result	Break Even	$0.00

There are many Break-Even calculators on the internet and you may even be able to make up your own. (The 'Management Toolbox has examples) As a decision making tool for owners and managers, it is unsurpassed. Once you start relying on it you will confidently make more sound decisions.

A couple of examples might help, 'if I want an office for my pen selling business and the rent will be $10.00 per week, how many pens do I have to sell to cover that cost?' And do I think that is reasonable? Can I do it?

'If I hire a bookkeeper and pay a salary of $20.00 per week, how many pens do I have to sell to cover that cost?" and do I think that is reasonable?

Using break-even as a decision making tool will help you make more sound decisions and you will do it confidently. You will know how much sales have to increase to pay for a new piece of equipment, or how much a new salesperson needs to bring in to pay for his position.

Your Business Track

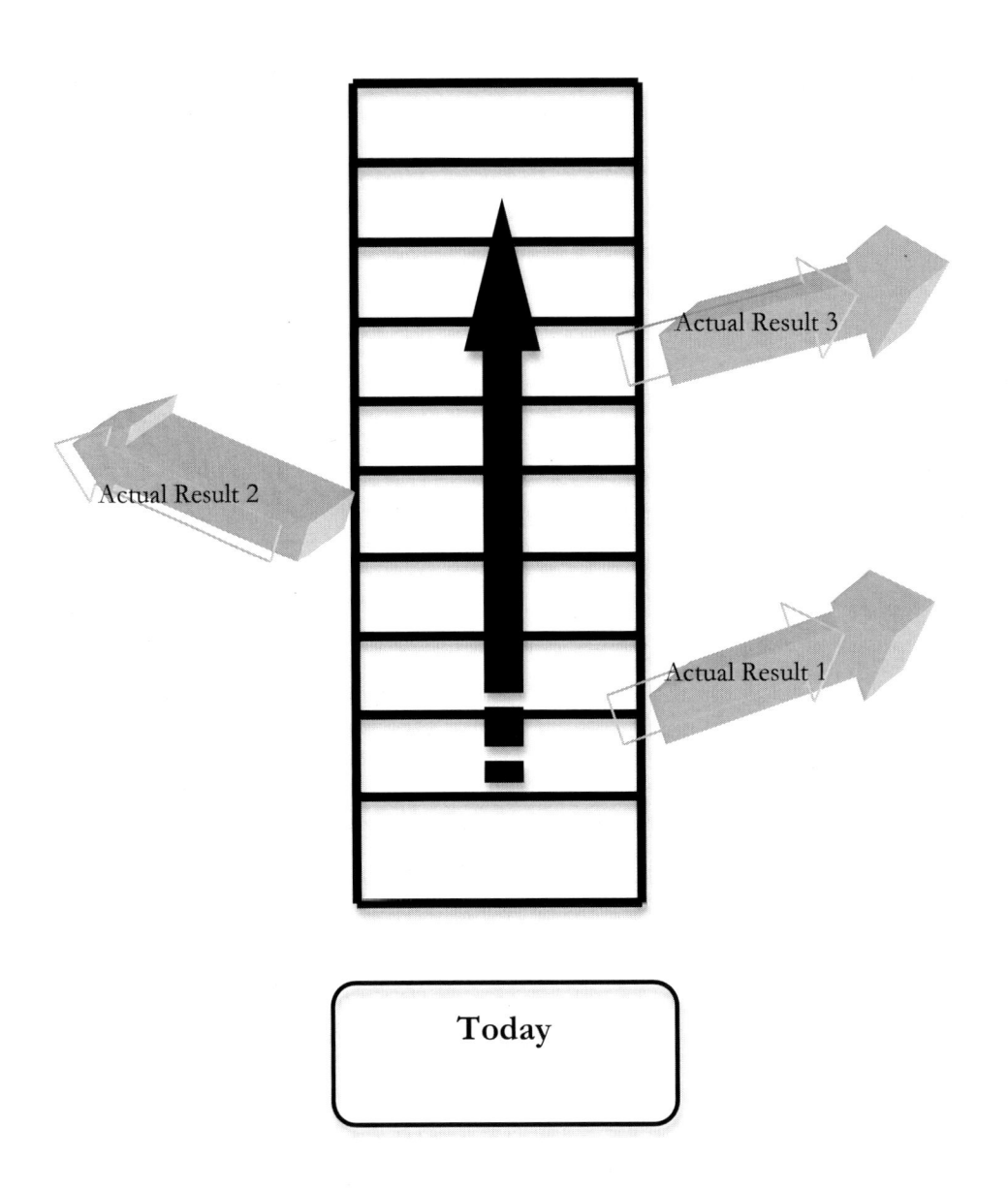

1 Year From Now!

Actual Result 3

Actual Result 2

Actual Result 1

Today

Step 4 – Laying Out Your Business Track

Many of you start jobs or projects with job drawings, architect blueprints or something that you or your clients have drawn. The point is you have a picture of what the end product or service looks like! And you then work towards that end.

You know this is perfectly logical and the only way it can work. But you have nothing like that for your own business. You don't think of it as building something. Remember the 'fatal assumption'.

Let's start with the present situation in which you find yourself. Imagine the track on the opposite page is a railway track.

- ➤ 'Today' on the track drawing on the opposite page is your present situation; good or bad, it represents where you are now!

- ➤ '1 Year From Now' at the top of the track is your goal for a specific time frame in the future. It may be one year, two years or three years down the road. I suggest it be set for one year for the first time. This text for '1 Year from Now' is difficult to see, or is unclear, because you probably don't have clear goals and most people don't. But if you consider them and make firm decisions as to what they are, the picture will clear up nicely so you can see your target.

    Sometimes people have a clear picture of where they are (the present situation) but no goals. You must have both in order to determine how to move down the track. If you don't know where you are and where you want to go, what are your chances of getting there?

- ➤ This step by step business track describes exactly what you will do in each area of your business to get from where you currently are, to where you want to be. You will learn to use specific management tools and to develop systems and controls to accomplish the appropriate tasks.

- ➤ Some people can describe the present situation and some can even do a fair job of describing where they want to be one year down the road. But when the end of the year arrives they are not at the top of the track nor have they achieved their goal. In fact they have ended up at one of the alternate smaller side tracks-- different from where they wanted to be-- and they don't know why!

> These alternatives are 'side tracks'. People often don't know they are on a side track until it's too late to do anything about it or to fix it. Again, this happens because they lack business systems and controls.

> To avoid this you need to have control switches (stop signs) that tell you when you are heading off track. Remember, you cannot manage what you do not measure. Control switches are things like budgets, cash flow projections, variance reports, personnel evaluations etc. You must be able to measure your progress in all areas of your business in a timely fashion.

Job progress stages or steps

If you are on a job that is scheduled for a specific time, say one month, and you are three weeks in and only 20 percent finished, do you have a problem? And if so, when would you like to know about the problem?

If you have used 60 percent of your labor budget and find yourself 30 percent complete, do you have a problem? And if so, when would you like to know about the problem?

If this logic is correct on the job site…it is also correct from your management perspective and you and I both know that. You must know the status of your work at various points in order to manage or control the outcome.

However many people, when considering a business due to the issues described above usually don't know the score until the game is over and when it's too late to take corrective action. They lost money and they don't know why. Just like baseball managers you need a system that gives you the information you need <u>while it is still useful</u>, so you can make changes to stay on track…

You Need A Business System.

Components Of A Business System

A business system is comprised of four basic areas and your action plan will have components in each area:

1. Sales or 'Getting The Work'
2. Organization or 'Doing The Work'
3. Financial Management or Measuring The Work'
4. Management or 'Controlling It All'

Our management 'ToolBox' has many tools that have been built and used by professional consultants all over North America. Each of the four areas above has tools specifically for your use and they are provided electronically with the purchase of this book. They are listed at the end of the book.

Building a business system should begin with the completion of a **S.W.O.T.** analysis **(strengths, weaknesses, opportunities, threats)**. What you're good at, your strengths, give rise to opportunities. What you're not good at, your weaknesses, pose threats to you and your business. You should be working to capitalize on your strengths and to improve your weaknesses. Putting them down on paper and recognizing them is the first step.

For example, you might be a great carpenter or engineer and are able to design and build a very high quality product. That's a strength. But, if you don't understand your costs and price the product so you lose money, that's a weakness. If you see a business that really needs the high quality product you have, that is an opportunity. If you have terrible sales skills and can't sell the product, that is a weakness. If your competition became aware of these weaknesses, they could pose a threat to the survival of your business. In each of these situations I am referring to it could be you, your people, your business location, your financial strength or lack thereof.

1. Sales or 'Getting The Work'

The sales strategies of the company must be determined with the objective of concentrating the sales efforts in the most profitable segments.

A good selling system has the following steps:

1. Identify to whom you're trying to sell (target markets)
   How many of them are there? Do you have more than one target?
   - How do you find leads now?
   - How else can you find leads?
   - What does it cost per lead?
   - What is the best method of finding leads?

2. Develop a sales process
   - Phone calls, letters, e-mail
   - How do you approach them and what do you say?
   - How do you move them toward a sale?
   - Do you have sales quotas? Should you?
   - Should you have sales territories?

3. Determine the necessary sales tools
   - Business cards, testimonials, web site, brochures etc.

4. Decide on the specific sales activities for your sales staff
   - Daily and weekly planning, regular time to make appointments, along with a step-by-step process of a sales call

5. Develop a method to track the above activities
   - Daily and weekly call reports to move the sales process forward

6. How do you compensate your sales people? Is it salary or commission? Which should it be?

A planned approach following this model will ensure a consistent approach to all customers and a standardized method of presentation. A sales and marketing system begins with your customer profile. This is a list of common characteristics of your average customer. It makes it easier to target them with advertising and sales activities. You can identify your target markets geographically, as well as by income level, sex, hobbies, marital status, home owners or renters etc. (and many more depending on the type of business). If you're selling to businesses you can categorize them by industry, size, number of employees etc.

You then set out the methods of best conveying your sales message to these target markets and how you will move towards closing sales.

To be effective your sales plan must be based on the A.I.D.A. principle. The acronym stands for:

- Attention
  - Before you can accomplish anything, people have to be:
    - listening to you
    - looking at you
    - reading your material
    - watching your ad
    - thinking about you

- Interest
  - Once you have their attention, you want them to:
    - picture themselves using or enjoying your product or service
    - imagine how their lives will be improved by your product or service
    - think about how your product or service will touch their families, business, their lives, their world in positive ways

- Desire
  - Continuing to work on the 'interest factors above' will create a desire for your products and services

- Action
  - The last and most critical step is to ask for action, or some type of commitment: the sales 'close'

Your sales efforts must move clients and customers through each of the four steps in order to succeed. This does not happen by accident, it needs detailed planning on your part.

2. Organization or 'Doing the Work'

The organization system describes how you plan to use the people at your disposal to accomplish your objectives (the HR system). You, as the owner or manager of a group need to set out specifically what you want your people to do...and how you want them to do it. After all, you're going to pay them to work for you, shouldn't you know what you expect them to do?

The most common complaint from employees is that they do not have a clear understanding of what is expected of them and that they have no idea about the direction of the company. These are communication and planning problems.

Most companies do not have a mission statement and many that do, have a very academic approach to this key tool. Your mission statement is the fundamental expression of your core values and is the basis of your leadership. It should not be longer than a few sentences and must be concise in order for your employees and customers to quickly grasp the meaning.

I have entered a client's offices many times to find a framed mission statement of several paragraphs on the wall. When I have removed it from the wall and asked the president to tell me what it said, they generally have great difficulty and can't do it! And if they don't know it, you can guess what the staff thinks of it, much less the customers.

The organization system sets out the basic business functions in a structure that shows lines of authority and communication, the organization chart. This chart sets out the positions required and the number of employees in various positions. You then describe exactly how the work is to be done in what are called job descriptions. If you don't have such itemized descriptions, employees will naturally do the job the way they think it should be done. What else would you expect? And how can you then rebuke or criticize them if you didn't tell them how to do it in the first place?

Job descriptions have four necessary components:

    1) a list of duties and responsibilities,
    2) a selection of which duties are to be measured, (80%-20% principle),
    3) an acceptable level of performance for those duties, and measurements,
    4) scope of authority for that position.

With this system in place you have control of what your employees do and therefore are able to channel their activities to more productive areas.

When you have agreement on the four points above you are putting yourself in a position to have employee accountability and responsibility. <u>Ownership and employees have the same expectations of the job and its outcome</u>.

With employee accountability you have control and therefore can ensure your business is moving in the right direction. This system applies to all administration, sales and operations functions.

Here is a true story that may help you understand the need for job descriptions. Those of you with kids will likely see this quicker than those without.

Many years ago when I was a junior consultant just getting started, I was part of a group presenting a two week program to 25 senior executives of a large international company. On Friday afternoon at the end of the first week we were talking about job descriptions and whether or not they were needed.

The group were all highly educated engineers and they were split right down the middle. One half thought job descriptions were a complete waste of time, after all they said, "we only hire intelligent people". The other half thought job descriptions were vital for proper communication and clarity of expectations.

At the end of the day we hadn't resolved the issue and agreed to carry it into the next week. Off we went to enjoy our weekends at home.

Saturday morning I was reading the newspaper and enjoying a cup of coffee when my son Chad came out of his bedroom. He was five years-old at the time. He asked if he could go play with Garnet, his best friend who lived across the street. I asked him, "Did you clean your room?", and he gave one of those shrugs that all parents instantly recognize that said, "ahhh busted". I of course, as the experienced parent, knew exactly what the shrug meant…he hadn't cleaned his room.

So I said, "Go and do it properly and then you can go play". Off he went, and a bit later he returned and said, "Can I go play now?"

I said, "Did you clean your room?" He said, "Yes". So I said, "Let me look!" And again I got another of those shrugs…guess what that meant?

"Go and do it properly and then you can go play!" I said emphatically. Off he went.

Well, this continued for a while and of course I never did go look. After four or five more times I said with a little frustration, "Oh, go ahead and go play, we'll finish that up later". He was out the door in an instant.

Not two minutes go by and Garnet's mother phones me and says while laughing, "You're a mean S.O.B today, what's going on over there?"

"Excuse me" I said, "What are you talking about?"

"Well" she said "Chad just came in and I asked him, "What have you been doing all morning?" Guess what he said? "Cleaning my room!"

"Hang on a minute" I said, "Let me go look". And so I did. And you all know exactly what I saw. The bedspread was thrown across the bed to cover up the mess underneath. His clothes were lying on the floor in the closet and toys were kicked under the bed.

He said he had been cleaning his room. Was he right?

Of course he was right. His room was clean…according to him!

But not according to me!

At that moment, I knew I had to relate this story to the group on Monday because now it was all so clear.

Job descriptions and workflow diagrams only exist for one reason. When you hire people you expect them to do certain activities in a specific way to accomplish a planned result. You must communicate that to them.

If you are not sure of what those activities are, how can they be sure?

If you do not make it crystal clear by writing them down and then teaching them how to do the job you're paying them to do…they will do it the way <u>they think it should be done</u>.

And that's okay if they happen to do it exactly as you wish. But what if they do it differently than the way you want it done?

If I don't teach my son how to make his bed, put his clothes away and put his toys away, can I say it's not properly done? Do I have a right to discipline him for not doing his job? Have I done *my* job?

Management is getting things done through other people.

If you own or manage a business it is your responsibility (your job) to ensure each person has the training and the tools to do their job properly. Each side (management and employee) needs to have a clear understanding of what is expected. Without a job description, this is next to impossible. And it leads to unproductive activities that cause profit leaks.

The story above also illustrates how to build an evaluation system into each job description. My son had three activities that I could easily evaluate:

1) make his bed
2) put his clothes away
3) put his toys away

If I judge each on a scale of 1-5 (5 being high) he has a possible score of 15. Now if he wants something extra, like special toys or activities or anything he wants, I can tie it to his evaluation. I might say a score of 12 is necessary for a certain reward, 10-12 might be a different reward, and 9 or less gets no reward. I can make this any way I like as long as he understands what is being judged and the rewards are something he wants.

I reward the activities and results I want by providing incentives he wants. This way I have a better chance of achieving what I want. Does it work all the time? Of course not, we're dealing with people here and it takes constant attention and creative thinking. But the results are a lot more positive than not having clarity of expectations.

Now if you look at an organization chart like the one on the next page, all you have to do is decide what each position needs to do in order to

"Clean their room"

Organization Chart

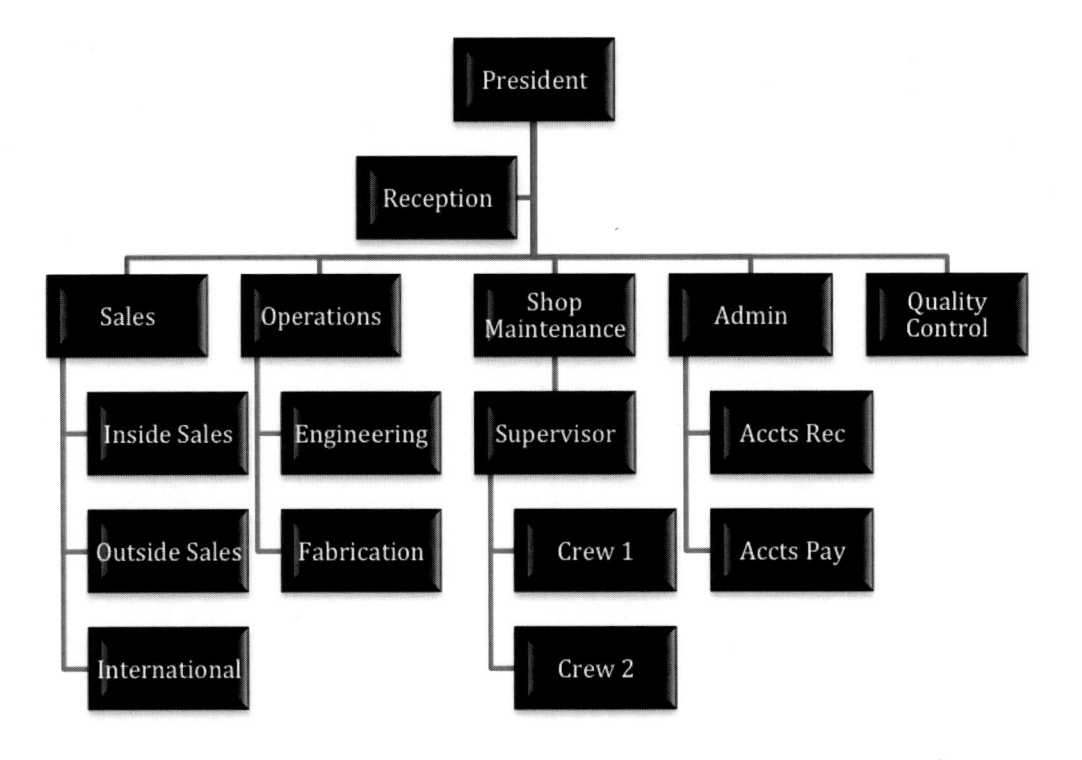

```
                          President
                             |
                         Reception
                             |
    ┌──────────┬──────────┬──┴──────────┬──────────┐
   Sales    Operations    Shop         Admin      Quality
                       Maintenance                Control
    │          │           │             │
 Inside     Engineering  Supervisor    Accts Rec
 Sales        │           │             │
    │       Fabrication  Crew 1        Accts Pay
 Outside                   │
 Sales                    Crew 2
    │
 International
```

The organization chart must be built around the functions that are necessary in the business, and not around the skills of the existing employees. It must and will constantly evolve as circumstances change. The purpose of the organization chart is to clearly set out the lines of authority and communication with-in the company.

Even though one person may wear many hats, each function must be identified so that you can clearly assign responsibility and authority for the tasks necessary to carry out that function.

3. Financial Management or 'Measuring the Work'

This is the scorekeeping system. Money is the measurement of business and you must be able to understand where you are at various points in the game. You don't need to become an accountant or a bookkeeper, but some fundamentals are required.

Earlier in our business track diagram we talked about a step-by-step system to accomplish your goals. You must remember to measure things in your business that cost you money. This measuring or scorekeeping system will tell you at the end of each specific step or time frame, how you are doing.

You must begin with a clear picture of where your revenue comes from.

Picture owning five coffee shops. You want to know how much of each product you sell from each shop, and what each product costs and how much you make on each product, in each shop! The revenue sources are called <u>revenue streams</u>.

You need to identify the different revenue streams in your business. For example it may be the type of business such as commercial or residential. It might be separated by location or city area. It might be wholesale and retail.

You must separate the direct or variable costs associated with that sale or type of sale. These direct costs have to be tracked apart from the administration or fixed costs in order to determine your gross profit by revenue stream. You then track the remaining costs such as your administration or fixed costs separately. Refer back to our Break-Even section. Most accounting systems will do this quite easily. Remember, you don't have to become an expert…just learn the fundamentals.

Once you have decided what to track, you need to estimate what the results should be over the next year. This is your financial operating plan. Now you have something to compare the actual results against; a baseline or benchmark.

On a small job or project for a client you likely have the estimate or budget you gave the client, or their budget. You have to complete the job as per the estimate or you will have an upset client, or you might not make any profit. This budget is your guideline, just as the financial operating plan is the guideline for your business. You need to know how to put one together and the track the results.

Contractors and builders have two major complaint areas; not on-time and not on-budget. This happens most of the time because they do not know their costs when they estimate and they are poor at scheduling and managing their labor.

There are four areas set out in the diagram below that provide an overall financial control and tracking system. This area, financial management, is by far the most common weakness in business owners and managers.

Manage By The Numbers

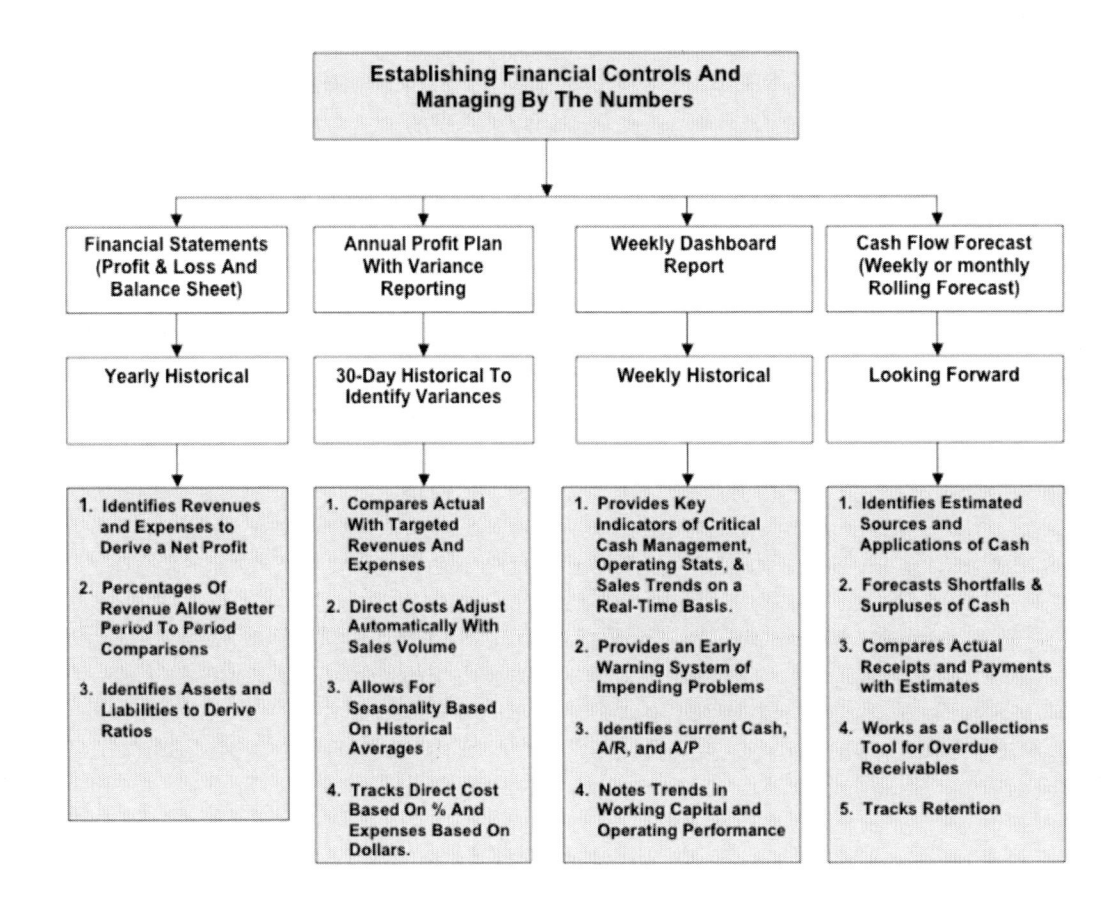

```
                    Establishing Financial Controls And
                       Managing By The Numbers
```

Financial Statements (Profit & Loss And Balance Sheet)	Annual Profit Plan With Variance Reporting	Weekly Dashboard Report	Cash Flow Forecast (Weekly or monthly Rolling Forecast)
Yearly Historical	30-Day Historical To Identify Variances	Weekly Historical	Looking Forward
1. Identifies Revenues and Expenses to Derive a Net Profit 2. Percentages Of Revenue Allow Better Period To Period Comparisons 3. Identifies Assets and Liabilities to Derive Ratios	1. Compares Actual With Targeted Revenues And Expenses 2. Direct Costs Adjust Automatically With Sales Volume 3. Allows For Seasonality Based On Historical Averages 4. Tracks Direct Cost Based On % And Expenses Based On Dollars.	1. Provides Key Indicators of Critical Cash Management, Operating Stats, & Sales Trends on a Real-Time Basis. 2. Provides an Early Warning System of Impending Problems 3. Identifies current Cash, A/R, and A/P 4. Notes Trends In Working Capital and Operating Performance	1. Identifies Estimated Sources and Applications of Cash 2. Forecasts Shortfalls & Surpluses of Cash 3. Compares Actual Receipts and Payments with Estimates 4. Works as a Collections Tool for Overdue Receivables 5. Tracks Retention

4. Management or 'Controlling It All'

In order to 'control' anything, you must have something to measure (activities) and something to measure it against (a budget or planned results, a baseline). When you know what it is you want to accomplish you can develop the appropriate measurement. Without a baseline the financial statements show you what happened, but you have nothing to compare it against, so you don't know if you should have done better. It's like having a dartboard for your business. Can you see the bulls-eye? What do you need to do to get closer and closer to it?

Having clear goals and objectives is the first step, setting priorities is the second and measuring progress is the third.

Your accounting system will produce a report showing the results of the operations after a period of time.

A 'dashboard report' is intended to measure the human activities that need to occur to produce positive results. It will be completed on a daily and weekly basis to provide information before the financial data is available. It will include activities that add to the value of your business or detract from it. The worksheet on the next page will provide the basis for setting goals with priorities and developing a 'Dashboard Report'.

The worksheet on the next page is a consultant's tool to help identify the limiting factors that are holding you back or preventing you from moving forward. Once a limiting factor or problem is identified you need to estimate the cost of the problem. This 'problem cost' will help determine priorities. The problem that costs you the most will likely be the highest priority and resolving it will lead to a large swing in the operational result.

For example, if a work crew of six mills around each morning for 20-30 minutes of paid time while the supervisor figures out what to do or where they are going. this is very poor people management and it has a significant problem cost!

Six men at 30 minutes each is three hours per day or 15 hours per week or 780 hours per year. If they were paid an average of $20 per hour that would be $15,600 per year without adding in the labor burden. If they work 7.5 hours per day they are wasting approximately seven percent of their time, or seven percent of your labor expense.

If you do not have enough sales because you are too busy doing other things but feel, that if you had the time, you could bring in another $1 million…then that is the problem cost.

Not doing it is costing you $1 million.

With a little guidance, you can complete the entire sheet and you may surprise yourself or scare yourself. The estimates that you jot down will help you easily identify the priorities or areas where you should start.

What's Holding You Back?

	What Holds You Back?	What's The Cost?	P	Activities	DashBoard Measurement Now Target	Impact in $ What If?
Get The Work Do you have enough sales? Could you handle more?				**Selling Function** -# of calls -# of quotes -ratio -sales per employee		
Do The Work How efficient are you? Could you do better? People capacity? Plant capacity?				**Workflow** -overtime hrs -scrap/waste time & materials -re-work, callbacks, opportunity cost -productivity rate -on-time delivery/shipping -machine utilization rate		
ScoreKeeping Get Paid Do you always have enough cash? Why not?				**Available Cash** -cash plan -days rec -days pay -days to invoice -days to deposit -discounts taken		
Measure The Work Making enough $? Understand B/E? Pricing?				**Cost Control** -use of budgets? -use of B/E -Inventory turnover -profit pricing -job costing -bad debts -budget to actual		
Control it all Do you feel in control?				**Control and Direction** -goals & objectives -profit needs identified -leadership -effective meetings -incentive plans		

Business Drivers

The worksheet on the previous page is used in many different formats by professional management consultants worldwide. Each and every business, regardless of the number of employees or the volume of sales has the same considerations:

1. **Get the work**
2. **Do the work**
3. **Get paid**
    a. **Measure the work**
4. **Control it all**

One method of setting goals is to determine what holds a business back or what restricts it from growing or doing better. It is the 'Business of Business' on a micro level. The presence or absence of these activities is what 'Drives' the value of a business up or down.

The worksheet is a guide and you may choose to use a full pad of paper for your own notes. I always start by talking to clients and asking them to tell me why they don't have more sales. Examine your situation and list the thoughts that you have in answer to this question. Often the answers relate to not having enough time to pursue more sales, or not knowing how to pursue more sales, or not having trained sales people.

The things that are holding you back have a cost, and once you know what is holding you back, you can estimate the cost of the problem. This then allows you to determine priorities. For example, if you think you could easily sell product worth another two million dollars with better trained sales people, <u>then not having trained sales people is now costing you two million dollars in revenue.</u>

Use the questions on the sheet as a starting point and complete the columns on What Holds You Back, What's The Cost and then set your own priorities. The dashboard is covered later on, but you may be able to estimate the impact of making the changes identified.

Why Don't People Reach Their Goals?

There are only three reasons people do not reach their goals:

1) They are unable
2) They are unwilling
3) They are inadequately trained

Which applies to you? Circle it above.

Don't assume that you know how to manage your business just because you understand the technical side.

Management is not rocket science and the system components can be learned. You don't have to learn them all at once. Start with the most critical items or areas where you are the weakest. Then just keep adding more skills as you are able.

Personal Action Plan

Depending on the present state of your business the action plan can vary from:

1) emergency measures in an attempt to survive, as described below, to

2) developing an overall management system with tools and controls.

Emergency Steps, or How To Get To A Survival Level

1. Manage cash flow to improve liquidity by immediately maximizing all cash generation opportunities including:
   a. review and accelerate accounts receivable collections
   b. review and decelerate accounts payable payments
   c. review and revise all personal requirements and payroll as necessary
   d. begin weekly completion of short term cash plan

2. Eliminate non-essential costs, personnel and non-core operations
   a. review Profit and Loss Statement line by line
   b. review balance sheet items line by line

3. Identify under performing operations and services
   a. review all revenue streams or product lines for profit contribution
   b. eliminate unacceptable streams or lines

4. Identify and accelerate the sale of existing or new products/services with optimum cash conversion cycles
   a. establish a selling process for identified products & services

5. Re-structure obligations to lenders and other creditors. Plan an approach to the above with the cash plan in mind and make a presentation that is in the interests of both parties. It should include short-term steps to be followed by a one year financial operating plan to be completed within a specific time frame.

6. <u>Plan a daily or weekly measuring/reporting process on each of the five steps above!</u>

7. Stabilize the overall business operation by consistently applying the above steps.

If the 'Emergency Steps' make sense when you're in trouble, wouldn't it make sense to follow them from day one!

If your business is doing well but you just want to learn to manage the company in a better way, or have someone else take a look and confirm you aren't missing something, then you might overlay the model of 'The Business of Business' on your company and identify the areas for improvement. Then begin to improve your own level of management skill.

Management System Components

The diagram on the opposite page has a list of the most common components used in each of the main management areas. They exist only to contribute to the overall company value. The higher the skill level you and your people have in each area the greater the contribution to the value of your company.

In the upper left corner are some of the more common goals listed by owners and managers. The important point to realize here is that those business goals are not the real goals...the personal goals in the right hand corner are examples of the real goals.

If you can clearly state your personal goals, it is then easier to state the business goals that will help you achieve what you really want.

Each of the listed components can then be implemented in your business to help you meet your business goals and by doing so, meet your personal goals.

The Business Of Business

Business Goals →
- Get Organized
- Understand Finance
- Get Control
- Profitability

← Personal Goals
- Have More Free Time
- Plan For Retirement
- Less Stress

Get The Work
- SWOT, Target Markets
- Sales Process, Tools, Reports, Training

Do The Work
- Workflow, Organization, Job Descriptions, Evaluations, Incentives, Compensation, Cross Training, Interviewing & Hiring, Orientation, Employee Handbook

Measure The Work
- Chart of Accounts, Breakeven, Overhead Ratio, Cash Flow, Labor Burden, Job Costing, Bidding/Estimating, Financial Operating Plan, Variance Reports, Inventory Control

Control It All
- Goals & Objectives, Consistent Purpose, Profit Needs, Continuous Improvement, Delegation, Effective Meeting, Decision Making, Management Reports

Policy Manual
- Planning, Policies, Analysis

Practical Tools For Practical People

Understanding Financial Statements

> *My experience has taught me that most business owners have very little knowledge in this area and place little importance on it. But once they learn a little, they almost always want more, so here are the first steps.*

The great majority of business owners and managers do not have a working knowledge of their financial statements because they have not put forth the effort, nor have they understood any reason to do so. For many people, 'crunching numbers' is an activity to be feared.

Some very common remarks are:

> "I'm in business to sell…not to be a bookkeeper."
> "That's what I pay my accountant for."
> "I could never learn that mumbo jumbo".

If you have one or more of these thoughts you are likely not maximizing your business profit. The fear you may experience comes from a lack of understanding. You do not have to become a bookkeeper, nor get rid of your accountant. And it's only mumbo jumbo until you understand some of the basic concepts.

You quite likely pay an accountant or a bookkeeper a substantial sum of money each year to keep track of your money. You should at least be able to understand the jargon. Try not to look at bookkeeping and accounting as crunching numbers but more as keeping track of money, *your money*! And if you're going to hire someone to do that, shouldn't you at least know a little about what they are doing? How else will you know if they're doing a good job?

Aside from the legal requirements to maintain financial records, there are internal management requirements for information that comes from financial records. Often people don't realize this until they get into trouble with their business.

Want to expand your inventory? How much do you need? Will the bank lend you the money? Is there a way you can determine this? Will you be able to pay your bills in the coming months? Can you take extra money out to buy your teenage son or daughter the car you promised? Can you put some away for your retirement? Do you want to feel like you are really in control? Are you building a business worth selling?

Sure, you can pay a professional to provide some of the answers, but it is your business.

Are you in control of it? Or is it in control of you?

Most business people think about doing their actual work in a very systematic way. They are used to that and they understand it. You can take the same systematic way of thinking and apply it to business. Business is a system and has specific tools to use. Understanding the financial side of business is just another system. Once you learn to use a few of the tools and you see the logical flow of the system, it's not difficult at all.

You need to keep financial records for legal reasons. You have to pay tax and you need reports in order to do so. But I think the more important reason is to make sure you accomplish what you set out to do.

You started a business because you had a dream, part of that requires making money. So I think that if you are going to run a business you might as well make as much money as you can. In order to do that you need to know if you are using equipment, people, inventory and debt in the best possible way. This means you need some measurement tools.

All financial statements really do is describe the things a business owns, how it got those things, what it owes and to whom, and where it spent its money. Can you answer those questions about your business?

These financial statements must be put together in a consistent manner. This manner is called the 'Generally Accepted Accounting Principles' (G.A.A.P.). Without these guidelines there could be no meaningful interpretation of the financial records of a company. Many of you will appreciate this from the following perspective. I have seen many companies hire a bookkeeper that has his or her own way of doing things. That person leaves and is replaced by another, and then another. Over a few years <u>several different ways</u> are jumbled together until the records are a complete mess and nothing makes any sense.

This happens because the owner has little understanding and therefore cannot give any direction to a very critical area of the company. Most bookkeepers understand some of the process of bookkeeping but very little about management. This causes huge problems when you present those statements to the bank, or you are simply trying to understand where all the money goes, and why you don't have more than you do.

People run a business to make money but then pay little or no attention to how they actually make money! *Does this make sense?*

The Balance Sheet

Let's start with the starting point. The accounting system is meant to track what you start with, what you do with it, and what you end up with. Let's look at a picture of what the company looked like on its first day.

> It's called a 'Balance Sheet'. It shows:
> 1) what you own, 2) what you owe, and 3) your share
>
> In business jargon that is:
> 1) the assets, 2) the liabilities, and 3) the equity

This is a picture of what the company has at that point in time (what you started with). It will change with the very next business transaction.

1) What you own. (The Assets)

These are all the things owned that have value. They can be tangible such as cash, amounts people owe you, or physical things like buildings, inventory, equipment, vehicles; or intangible things such as insurance bought and paid for in advance (prepaid insurance), copyrights, patents and goodwill.

These assets are divided into categories.

> Current assets are listed first and are in order of 'liquidity' or nearness to cash. They are things that in the normal course of your business will be converted to cash in the current business year. That's why they are called 'current assets.
>
> Example:
>
> Cash
> Account Receivable
> Inventory
> Prepaid Postage
>
> Cash means cash on hand. The total of all sources, petty cash plus what's in the bank.

Fixed Assets are the physical properties or pieces of equipment that a company uses to support its business but does not sell in the normal course of business. They generally have a life span of several years and are listed in order of durability or life span. Land is first, followed by buildings, equipment etc. Similar items are collected under one heading.

Items are listed at their historical cost, that is, what was paid for them. If you tried to list them at current market value you could only use estimates, and ten people would have ten different estimates. By using historical cost, everyone is able to understand what he or she is reading when looking at the fixed asset section of a balance sheet.

Because these assets contribute to the earning power of a business for several years, it makes sense to allocate part of their cost to each year the asset helps you earn income. This allocation is called depreciation and is an expense for each individual year it is claimed. On your balance sheet you will see 'accumulated depreciation' for fixed assets. This is simply the sum of the depreciation claimed over the years of the asset's lifespan to date.

The difference between the historical cost and the accumulated depreciation is called the 'net book value'. This is a paper value only and has nothing to do with the asset's market value. This is done in order to accurately match the costs of doing business with the resulting revenues for a specific period of time.

Land		$75,000
Buildings	$200,000	
Less Accumulated Depreciation	($40,000)	$160,000
Equipment	$40,000	
Less Accumulated Depreciation	($8,000)	$32,000
Vehicles	$35,000	
Less Accumulated Depreciation	($10,000)	$25,000

Remember, the net book value is for accounting purposes only, and does not indicate market value. If you are buying or selling a business, you must determine the market value independently.

Other Assets

A third category of assets you may run across is 'Other Assets'. This is where you will find the costs of incorporation, patents, copyrights and goodwill.

If you started your business then you won't find goodwill on your balance sheet. But you probably think your business is worth more that the cost of the assets. This is the value of your reputation or ability to earn profit. It is the difference between the dollar value of your assets and what a buyer would be willing to pay for your business. This is 'Goodwill' and it will appear on the buyer's balance sheet if he or she buys your business. Remember the principle of 'Historical Cost'. Goodwill is something purchased by the buyer.

Current Assets			
Cash		$3,200.00	
Accounts Receivable		$18,200.00	
Inventory		$15,000.00	
Prepaid Expenses		$2,000.00	
Total Current Assets			$38,400.00
Fixed Assets			
Land		$45,000.00	
Buildings	$82,000.00		
Less - Accumulated Depreciation	-$16,000.00	$66,000.00	
Equipment	$25,000.00		
Less - Accumulated Depreciation	-$8,500.00	$16,500.00	
Vehicles			
Less - Accumulated Depreciation	$32,000.00		
	-$10,500.00	$21,500.00	
Total Fixed Assets			$149,000.00
Other Assets			
Goodwill		$15,000.00	
Patents		$25,000.00	
Total Other Assets			$40,000.00
Total Assets			**$227,400.00**

2) Liabilities

All the things a business owes are divided into categories just like the assets. They are listed in order of when they must be paid. Current liabilities are listed first because they are due in the current business year.

Example:
>	Current Liabilities
>>		-Demand Loan
>>		-Accounts Payable
>>		-Income Taxes payable
>>		-Current Portion of Long-Term Debt
>	Total Current Liabilities

A demand loan is payable on demand, and therefore is listed first. The current portion of long-term debt is the amount of principal that must be paid in the next twelve months or in the current business year. A five-year loan with monthly payments of $1,000 plus interest would have a current portion of $12,000. The total current liabilities are what must be paid within one year.

Long Term Liabilities are those debts that will remain at the end of the current business year. These are generally equipment loans and mortgages.

Example
>	Long-Term Liabilities
>>		-Vehicle Loan
>>		-Building Mortgage
>>>			Less current Portion
>>		-Total Long Term Liabilities

3) The last category of liability is what is owed to the owners of the company. It is called equity or capital. It refers to the amount left after other liabilities are deducted from the total assets. If your balance sheet shows a heading called 'Retained Earnings', it is the amount of profit you have left in the company in the past. If the business has had significant losses, this equity section may be a negative number.

Many owners plan to retire and use their equity to fund that retirement. If that is you, then you need to understand how to read this section and interpret it to ensure an adequate supply of funds when needed.

Current Liabilities		
Demand Loan	$5,000.00	
Accounts Payable	$8,000.00	
Income Taxes Payable	.00	
Current Portion Of Long-Term Debt	$11,000.00	
Total Current Liabilities		$24,000.00
Long-Term Liabilities		
Term Loans	$109,000.00	
-Less Current Portion Above	-$11,000.00	
Total Long-Term Debt		$98,000.00
Owner's (Shareholders) Equity		
Capital Stock	$75,000.00	
Retained Earnings	$5,400.00	
Total Owner's Equity		$80.400.00
Total Liabilities and Owner's Equity		$202,400.00

Each category is sub-totaled and then totaled at the bottom. The 'Equity' section is the liability or what the business or company owes to the owners. The total assets will always equal the total liabilities and owners equity. This is sometimes referred to as the basic accounting equation:

$$\text{Assets} = \text{Liabilities} + \text{Owners Equity}$$

Even if the business is bankrupt, this equation will be true. The equity section would then be a negative number because the business has less than it owes.

To reinforce what you have read and to help apply the concepts to your company I have included an exercise you should do prior to examining your own statements.

Balance Sheet Exercise

Exercise 1 – place the accounts and the corresponding amounts from the list below into the appropriate balance sheet order on the next page.

Accumulated Depreciation	$16,000.00
Accounts Payable (A/P)	$8,000.00
Inventory	$15,000.00
Goodwill	$15,000.00
Land	$45,000.00
Demand Loan	$5,000.00
Accounts Receivable (A/R)	$18,200.00
Vehicles	$32,000.00
Term Loan	$109,000.00
Accumulated Depreciation (Equip)	$8,500.00
Accumulated Depreciation (Vehicles)	$10,500.00
Current Portion of Long-Term Debt	$11,000.00
Cash	$3,200.00
Capital Stock	$75,000.00
Total Current Assets	$38,400.00
Total Current Liabilities	$24,000.00
Total Fixed Assets	$149,000.00
Retained Earnings	$5,400.00
Total Equity	$80,400.00
Prepaid Expenses	$2,000.00
Buildings	$82,000.00
Equipment	$25,000.00

Balance Sheet Exercise – Answer Sheet

Etch-A-Sketch Management Company Inc.

Balance Sheet

As At December 31, 2010

Assets			Liabilities		
Current Assets			**Current Liabilities**		
Cash			Demand Loan		
Accounts Receivable			Accounts Payable		
Inventory			Current Portion		
Prepaid Expenses					
Total Current Assets			**Total Current Liabilities**		
Fixed Assets			**Long-Term Liabilities**		
Land			Term Loan		
Buildings			Less current portion		
Acc Depreciation					
Vehicles			**Total Long-Term Liabilities**		
Acc Depreciation			**Equity**		
Equipment			Capittal Stock		
Acc Depreciation			Retained Earnings		
Total Fixed Assets			**Total Equity**		
Other Assets					
Goodwill					
Total Other Assets					
Total Assets			**Total Liabilities & Equity**		

Completed Version of the Balance Sheet Exercise

Etch-A-Sketch Management Company Inc.

Balance Sheet

As At December 31, 2010

Assets			Liabilities		
Current Assets			**Current Liabilities**		
Cash	$3,200		Demand Loan	$5,000	
Accounts Receivable	$18,200		Accounts Payable	$8,000	
Inventory	$15,000		Current Portion	$11,000	
Prepaid Expenses	$2,000				
Total Current Assets		$38,400	**Total Current Liabilities**		$24,000
Fixed Assets			**Long-Term Liabilities**		
Land		$45,000	Term Loan	$109,000	
Buildings	$82,000		Less current portion	-$11,000	
Acc Depreciation	-$16,000	$66,000			
Vehicles	$32,000		**Total Long-Term Liabilities**		$98,000
Acc Depreciation	-$10,500	$21,500	**Equity**		
Equipment	$25,000		Capital Stock	$75,000	
Acc Depreciation	-$8,500	$16,500	Retained Earnings	$5,400	
Total Fixed Assets		$149,000			
Other Assets			**Total Equity**		$80,400
Goodwill	$15,000				
Total Other Assets		$15,000			
Total Assets		$202,400	**Total Liabilities & Equity**		$202,400

Income Statement Exercise

Place the items below in the proper Income Statement format on the next page and calculate the subtotals and totals.

General Expenses	$45,000.00
Purchases	$250,000.00
Opening Inventory	$110,000.00
Gross Sales	$480,000.00
Ending Inventory	$115,000.00
Administrative Expenses	$40,000.00
Returns and Allowances	$15,000.00
Selling Expenses	$65,000.00

Income Statement Exercise – Answer Sheet

Etch-A-Sketch Management Company Inc.

Income Statement

For The Year Ended December 31, 2010

Sales		
Less Returns and Allowances		
Net Sales		
Cost of Goods/Services Sold		
Opening Inventory		
Plus Purchases		
COG Available for sale		
Less Ending Inventory		
Total Cost of Goods/Services Sold		
Gross Profit		
General and Administrative Expenses		
General		
Administrative		
Selling		
Total G & A Expenses		
Income/Loss From Operations		

Income Statement Completed Answer Sheet

Etch-A-Sketch Management Company Inc.
Income Statement
For The Year Ended December 31, 2010

Sales	$480,000	
Less Returns and Allowances	15,000	
Net Sales		$465,000
Cost of Goods/Services Sold		
Opening Inventory	$110,000	
Plus Purchases	250,000	
COG Available for sale	360,000	
Less Ending Inventory	-115,000	
Total Cost of Goods/Services Sold		$245,000
Gross Profit		$220,000
General and Administrative Expenses		
General	$45,000	
Administrative	40,000	
Selling	65,000	
Total G & A Expenses		$150,000
Income/Loss From Operations		$70,000

This purpose of this statement is to record the revenue and the costs of generating that revenue for a specific period. It is called many things; a Statement Of Revenue And Expenses, a Profit and Loss Statement and a P & L Statement. They all mean the same thing. When you prepare one in advance, that is, looking ahead, it is called an operating budget. It is completed to provide direction and to give you a benchmark against which to measure the actual results. The comparison allows trends to be identified so early corrective action can be undertaken in time to affect the end result. Look at the next example and imagine having yours prepared in a similar fashion for the year ahead. Then at the end of each month being able to compare what you had planned to do with what you actually did.

Etch-A-Sketch Management Company Inc.
Projected Income Statement
For The Year Ended December 31, 20___

Sales	$480,000	
Less Returns and Allowances	15,000	
Net Sales	$465,000	100%
Cost of Goods/Services Sold		
Opening Inventory	$110,000	23.7%
Plus Purchases	250,000	53,8%
COG Available for sale	360,000	77.4%
Less Ending Inventory	-115,000	
Total Cost of Goods/Services Sold	$245,000	52.7%
Gross Profit	$220,000	47.3%
General and Administrative Expenses		
General	$45,000	9.7%
Administrative	40,000	8.6%
Selling	65,000	14.0%
Total G & A Expenses	$150,000	32.3%
Income/Loss From Operations	$70,000	15.1%

Etch-A-Sketch Management Company Inc.
Month End P & L Report - Planned vs Actual
For The Month Ended January 31, 20___

	Budget		Actual	
Sales	$55,000		$59,400	
Less Returns				
Net Sales	$55,000	100%	$59,400	100%
Cost of Goods/Services Sold				
Opening Inventory	$110,000		$110,000	
Plus Purchases			0	
COG Available for Sale	$110,000		$110,000	
Less Ending Inventory	$86,000		$86,000	
Total Cost of Goods/Services Sold	$24,000	43.6%	$24,000	40.4%
Gross Profit	$31,000	56.4%	$35,400	59.6%
General and Administrative Expenses				
General	$3,800	6.3%	$4,100	6.9%
Administrative	$5,200	9.5%	$5,450	9.2%
Selling	$7,000	12.7%	$8,500	14.3%
Total G & A Expenses	$16,000	29.1%	$18,050	30.4%
Income/Loss From Operations	$15,000	27.3%	$17,350	29.2%

Sales are given the value of 100% and all other costs are expressed as a percentage of that number. The purchasing power of a dollar changes constantly so we want to be able to make stable comparisons over time. This format allows you to do that.

Now take a look at your in-house prepared statement. Does it make more sense? How often do you look at your score sheet? Do you want it to give you more information?

While you will hear about other items included in the 'Financial Statements', these two; the Balance Sheet and the Income Statement or the P & L (Profit and Loss) are of major concern to you in terms of management tools.

While they are both important and provide different information, there are some links between the two. I always coach people to concentrate on the Income Statement until they have solid grasp of it. Then include the Balance Sheet.

Many companies have in-house bookkeepers that are skilled at bookkeeping but are not able to produce these statements accurately because they do not understand accounting. Of course, they don't tell you that. And you the owner, not knowing what to expect, don't understand what they show you. The statement may show that you made a profit, <u>but you don't know where the money is</u>! And it's certainly not in the bank.

These businesses then must take their records to an outside accounting firm for tax preparation. Often, these firms simply rebuild the records from bank statements, invoices and paid bills, receipts and other original documents that you provide because they have learned that it's faster than trying to figure out what the bookkeeper tried to do.

However; there is a time lag between the occurrence of business activities or events and the appearance of the results in the financial statements. This can be several weeks or even months. I have had many owners tell me they see the financials every year when the accountant prepares them. They know this is wrong, but they don't know what to do about it.

Wouldn't you rather know how you're doing as you're doing it?

The 'Dashboard' Report

The purpose of the 'Dashboard Report' is to provide you with information about what's going on in critical areas prior to the availability of the financial reports. It is intended to track people activities, and to ensure they are doing what they are supposed to be doing.

The key areas are sales, operations, people and finance. The individuals in charge of these areas have specific activities that lead to both positive and negative results.

<u>Sales</u> - people need to make calls, go to appointments, make presentations and track progress towards closing sales. They need to find new clients, maximize sales to existing clients or customers.

<u>Operations</u> - needs to actually do the work, package materials, schedule and install, make sure people are at the right place at the right time with the right materials and control re-work.

<u>People</u> - need to be at work on schedule in sufficient numbers, with sufficient training, complete tasks on time, control mistakes, and be safe.

<u>Finance</u> – a business needs to maximize the cash available to it. So deposits need to be made in a timely manner, receivables collected on time, discounts taken when appropriate, bills paid promptly but not early, invoices sent promptly, prices calculated profitably and updated regularly.

Many of these activities can be tracked with little paper work and reported on a weekly basis so you know things are happening the way they are designed to happen. If all these activities are moving in a positive way, the financial results will be as expected, but if they are negative, you don't need to wait for the financial results to tell you that.

Management is expected to manage the business so that means measuring activities. The sooner you know about negative activities the sooner you can take corrective action.

If you can't measure it, you can't manage it!

Sample Dashboard Report

Sales			Operations	
	Planned	Actual		
# of calls			Scrap (time or materials)	
# of appts			Re-work hours	
# of new clients			Productivity rate	
# of estimates			Machine utilization	
Estimate to Award Ratio			On time ship rate	
People			Finance	
Vacation			Cash on Hand	
Absence			Days Receivable	
Lost Hours			Days payable	
Overtime Hours			Payroll	
			Revenue per employee	

Use this format as a guide. Don't go overboard and list too many things. The purpose of this report is to mimic your car or truck's dashboard. If someone put a blanket over your dashboard, it would be difficult or impossible to drive.

You don't need to understand the internal working of your car or truck's engine to know if it's running right. The gauges on the dashboard tell you if there is a problem so then you can check it out. This is the same approach.

We build a gauge to tell you how each major function is working. If the needle is pointing in the wrong direction, then you need to dig deeper. Otherwise, if you have properly planned the activities that should be occurring in each function, and they are happening according to plan, everything should be fine.

Conclusion

My years of travel and work experience with hundreds of different businesses all over North America have taught me that while most owners believe they are somewhat unique and that their business really is different from others...

...it's just not true.

Sure, the technical part may well be new and unique, but the concepts of running a successful business and making money are universal.

Every business must produce more resources than it consumes. I am certain that all of you will agree with the logic in the 'emergency steps' listed on the previous page. If they are logical when a business is on its last legs in order to save it...imagine following those steps from day one in your business.

Management is a skill, and as such it is learnable and transferable from one to another. It takes discipline and hard work, but then, you're working anyway aren't you?

Why not work the most productive way possible?

Now, having said all that...you need to recognize if you are trying to run a business, or are running a business, you are part of a very special segment of our society. There are three kinds of people in our world:

> **1) those who make things happen**
>
> **2) those who criticize what happens**
>
> **3) those who wonder what happened**

You are part of the first group, a very small group, a very special group. Many of you try again and again and again. You climb up and fall down, sometimes you're knocked down, but you get up, you climb up again and again and again!

You are to be admired because you create! And because you don't give up! People depend on you for jobs and income to support their families. You make their lives what they are.

The second group just criticizes. Know anyone like that? It's the easiest thing in the world. They never do anything, but they sure know how to poke holes in what other people do. You need to learn to ignore them.

The third group just floats through life wondering what's going on. You might have some of them working for you.

In Acapulco, the cliff divers have to jump off at the top without being able to see the water. All they can see from the top are rocks, but they still jump, they believe they can make it. Just like business entrepreneurs, they believe they can make it, so they jump.

So use all the planning and tools that are available to you, but recognize that you can't plan forever, nor can you have the perfect plan…and you still have to

just jump!

The Manager's Tool-Box

The Manager's Tool-Box is comprised of an ever changing set of management tools. Some are step-by-step instructions written in Microsoft Word in layman's terms and some are Microsoft Excel Spreadsheet tools to assist in calculations. Both are examples of what should be everyday tools for owners and managers. They are the result of many years of working with hundreds of business clients in all industries all over North America. Some you will like more than others.

As you identify things you want to learn, search for it in the Tool-Box. If you are looking for something and can't find it, let me know. Perhaps it is in development now or should be. I appreciate any suggestions. You learn at your own pace and I am here to help with any difficulties you may have.

While the entire Tool-Box is available on my website, you may want some help in certain areas. The regular price for this type of coaching can be quite expensive, but if you are capable of using the Internet, and something like Skype or I-Chat to communicate with me, you can save a significant amount of money. This eliminates the need for travel expenses and still provides face-to-face contact between you and I.

I provide blocks of coaching time in 10 hour increments at prices you can afford. This is very helpful if you are really pressed for time or find yourself in really bad circumstances.

Contact me at: www.practicalbusinesscoach.com

The Manager's Tool-Box

1. Getting Ready
    a. Before You Buy a Business!
    b. Authority, Responsibility and Accountability
    c. Evaluating A Business Idea
    d. Evaluating Your Business
    e. The Management Process
    f. Personal Direction Questionnaire
    g. Goals and Objectives Worksheets

2. Organization
    a. Purpose and Mission Statement
    b. Functional Organization Chart
    c. Position Guides or Job Descriptions
        i. Task Guides
    d. Employment Agreement
    e. Evaluation System
    f. Incentive or Profit Sharing Plans

3. Sales and Marketing
    a. Introduction to Marketing
    b. Cold Call Selling
    c. Relationship Selling
    d. Negotiations
    e. Advertising And Promotions
    f. Effective Business Presentations
    g. Tactical Sales Forms

4. Personnel
    a. Behavioral Interviewing
    b. Developing And Assessing Training Plans
    c. Discipline Without Punishment
    d. Employee Orientation
    e. Progressive Discipline
    f. Supervision
    g. Team building
    h. Training Adults
    i. Motivation
    j. Employee Handbook

5. Finance
    a. Chart Of Accounts
    b. Credit and Collections
    c. Income and Expense Review
    d. Introduction To Financial Statements
    e. Labor Burden Canada
    f. Labor Burden US
    g. Overhead Allocation
    h. Cash Flow Projection
    i. Flexible Budget With Break-Even and Cash Flow
    j. Understanding Break-Even
    k. Break-Even Calculator
    l. Sales commission Calculator

6. General
    a. Creative Thinking
    b. Conflict Management
    c. Decision Making
    d. Effective Business Meetings
    e. Effective Delegation
    f. Leadership
    g. Managing Change
    h. Problem Solving
    i. Stress Management
    j. Succession Planning
    k. Quality Management

7. Construction Industry
    a. Bid Preparation and Job Costing
    b. Job Opening Procedure
    c. Job Closing Procedure
    d. Change Order Format
    e. Introduction to Job Costing
    f. Introduction To Project Planning
    g. Equipment Cost Calculator (cost per hour and cost per mile)

The Business Of Business

SUCCESS

What's On The Horizon For Your Business?

Ronald La Fournie